Cambridge Studies in Social Anthropology

General Editor: Jack Goody

17

PRODUCTION AND REPRODUCTION

OTHER TITLES IN THE SERIES

CAMBRIDGE PAPERS IN SOCIAL ANTHROPOLOGY

PRODUCTION AND REPRODUCTION

A COMPARATIVE STUDY OF THE DOMESTIC DOMAIN

JACK GOODY

CAMBRIDGE UNIVERSITY PRESS

CAMBRIDGE
LONDON · NEW YORK · MELBOURNE

Published by the Syndics of the Cambridge University Press
The Pitt Building, Trumpington Street, Cambridge CB2 1RP
Bentley House, 200 Euston Road, London NW1 2DB
32 East 57th Street, New York, NY 10022, USA
296 Beaconsfield Parade, Middle Park, Melbourne 3206, Australia

© Cambridge University Press 1976

Library of Congress catalogue card number: 76-4238

ISBN 0 521 21294 4 hard covers
ISBN 0 521 29088 0 paperback

First published 1976

Photoset and printed in Malta by Interprint (Malta) Ltd

To Mary and to Rachel

Contents

Tables

Figures

Preface

When I first took a berth on boat to West Africa, I did not do so with the sole purpose of getting to know something about an African society or, more generally, the 'savage mind.' I was certainly very involved with the problems of getting to know another culture, another way of looking at the world. But other concerns were present too. What I knew of the medieval literature and history of Europe whetted my appetite to learn more about pre-industrial societies, their beliefs as well as their economic and productive systems. A period in the eastern Mediterranean had extended these interests in time and in space.

Secondly, there was the immediate situation in which I found myself in West Africa. Events were moving fast in Ghana during the period I was first there and the Convention People's Party, to the Birifu branch of which I was inscribed, were well on their way to power. However it was not only the links between local 'tribe' and national politics that concerned me, but the earlier links, with long distance trade, with Islam, with neighbouring states. It was on these historical subjects that I wrote when I first returned, and it was these subjects, in a wider context, that I pursued when trying to ask what it was that writers meant when they used terms like feudal to describe African states. How did the states and local communities in Ghana resemble and differ from those of Europe, Asia and the Middle East with which they were so often compared and contrasted? How could we best understand the differences between a village in the Italian Abruzzi and a settlement in Northern Ghana? What made people think the adjectives 'tribal', 'primitive', 'savage' appropriate to one set of cultures and not to the other? Were there no better ways of assessing similarity and difference than by means of a pair of crude binary oppositions?

Thirdly my interest in the Third World, in 'other cultures', had been stimulated by personal, political and social encounters in Africa and Europe during and after the Second World War. How could one bring a wider range of knowledge about these other societies to bear upon an understanding of our own situation? How could we provide historical, sociological, and humanistic studies generally, with a more universalistic base, a less European-centred framework?

To such very general questions, this book provides little by way of answers. What could? I introduce this personal note only by way of explaining an undertaking that may be thought to fall between a number of stools, those representing different academic fields of enquiry, different techniques of investigation, and different ways of understanding. As far as the first is concerned, the overlapping interests of those who study the wider aspects of human action, whether historians, sociologists or anthropologists, become increasingly obvious, despite the diverging tendencies of existing curricula and established departments, combined with worries of teachers and students who get uneasy when their boundaries tend to dissolve. As for techniques, by looking at a wider range of society, I have tried to assess hypotheses that were partly developed in intensive studies of a particular people. In order to carry out this larger enterprise, I have made use not only of the impressionistic methods usually adopted by comparative historians and sociologists when they get outside their own particular terrain, but I have also turned to the modern equivalent of an instrument used by some earlier scholars, namely a set of data drawn from a sample of world societies and recorded in the *Ethnographic Atlas*. This tool is seen as a way of supplementing, not replacing other methods of examining hypotheses. With all its drawbacks, it is an approach that permits of more systematic model building, because one can apply some kinds of validating procedures to the models, which are not simply there (as so often) to break up the print on the page. My use of these procedures is essentially tentative and exploratory. It attempts to give some concrete embodiment to a desire to test the ideas, theories and suggestions, that derive from interests in a particular society at a particular moment in time (which of course in turn emerge from the experience we initially bring to that situation) upon a wider canvas and (where possible) by more systematic methods. It is time we tried to fit together the numerous detailed investigations of social life in different parts of the world with the larger speculations on the development of human culture.

Acknowledgements

I begin the first chapter with a reference to the activities of 'The Edinburgh Evening Club', partly because the opportunity to consider the general trend of this research was presented to me by an invitation to deliver the Monro lectures in Edinburgh in 1972. It was not only the place but the scope of the activity of this group that was sympathetic. Here was a situation where lawyers, theologians, historians, philosophers, were all able to talk about the general and particular features of human societies in their transformations over time and space, with particular reference of course, to that range of society variously referred to as pre-capitalist, non-literate, simple(r), etc.

Apart from the reading in the general field of 'peasant' and African studies that has gone to the making of this book, I have had to rely upon the assistance of others to help with the more systematic aspects of the enquiry. Primarily I must thank the Social Science Research Council, London, whose Anthropological Sub-Committee generously supported a project which I suspect few regarded with much relish, namely the use of electronic data-processing techniques and elementary numerical procedures to analyse information abstracted from reports on a range of world societies. Of course material of this kind does violence to the rich particularity of each society – and of the constituent individuals. But so does any generalisation we make (and we make many in the course of an hour's conversation) on the basis of less reliable, less systematic impressions. In any case I have in no sense rejected the one in favour of the other; I have spent too long immersed in the intimacy of fieldwork situations to be tempted into the fruitless advocacy of one technique or approach as *against* another, characteristic as this procedure is of much of social science.

In the numerical analyses a number of people have helped me, notably my research assistants, Mrs L. March and Joan Buckley (who made the major contribution), to which I should add the names of Barrie Irving, Nickie Tahany, Graham Harrison, Ian Beeson, Dyanne Grant, Colin Duly, Clyde Mitchell and members of the staff of the Departments of Applied Economics and of Statistics of the University of Cambridge. Of course the hypotheses and discussion owe something to scholars in Cambridge and elsewhere, and perhaps I may thank them collectively for the chance remark, the critical comment, the odd reference, in case I have failed to acknowledge their help or opposition in more specific and courteous ways. For more general comments I am indebted to John Dunn, Robert Launay, and especially to Esther Goody.

Some of the material in this book has already appeared in print in various forms, because I did not want to wait until I had completed all the aspects of my enquiry before publishing some of the results. Needless to say, given such a broad canvas, the present volume is only a sketch of what might be done. In particular, I had intended to expand greatly the chapter on the structure of roles which I have entitled 'Concubines and Co-Wives' by dealing with systematic differences in other relationships. But involved in other matters, I have not had the time to develop the notes that I had made.

The earlier chapters deal with the attempt to offer more systematic comparisons. I have presented the substantial argument in the text while placing the more detailed numerical material in the Appendices. The second chapter contains an analysis of the distribution and correlations of the relevant variables found in the *Ethnographic Atlas*, the original report appearing as 'Inheritance, property and marriage in Africa and Eurasia', *Sociology*, 3 (1969), 55–76. The figures presented here have been slightly amended as the result of subsequent changes in the Atlas and of rechecking the deck of punched cards, a final version of which is deposited with the SSRC Data Bank, University of Essex, Wivenhoe Park, Colchester, Essex. The following chapter, based upon an article written in collaboration with Barrie Irving and Nickie Tahany (1971), attempts to apply linkage and path analysis to the data discussed in the previous section; and in the fourth, I introduce a variable omitted from the earlier work but the relevance of which is brought out very clearly in Ester Boserup's book, *The Role of Women in Economic Development* (1970): in this section, which was written in collaboration with Joan Buckley and was first presented as a paper to the Oxford meeting of the Association of Social Anthropologists in July 1973, we attempt to integrate a consideration of male and female roles in the division of labour with the rest of the analysis.

Other material that has appeared in print is as follows:

Chapter 6. Derived from 'Adoption in cross-cultural perspective', *Comparative Studies in Society and History*, 11 (1969), 55–78.

Chapter 7. From 'Strategies of heirship', *Comparative Studies in Society and History*, 15 (1973), 3–20.

Chapter 8. 'Class and marriage in Africa and Eurasia', *American Journal of Sociology*, 76 (1971), 585–603.

Finally, it was an invitation from the Ecole des Hautes Études en Sciences Sociales, Paris, for the months of March to June, 1975, together with the hospitality of Pierre and Madeleine Smith, Françoise Héritier, Marc Augé and an attic room in Reid Hall, that enabled me to pull these various strands together into a single manuscript.

JACK GOODY

Cambridge, January 1976

1. The evolution of the domestic economy: the hoe and the plough

Just over 100 years ago, Edinburgh was the location of a series of important developments in the field of comparative sociology. Much of this activity centred around the publishing house of Black, the production of the *Encyclopedia Britannica* and around certain literary societies. One of the leading figures in this intellectual movement was the Cambridge-trained lawyer, J. F. McLennan (1827–81).[1] One of the men he influenced was W. Robertson Smith who also belonged to 'The Edinburgh Evening Club', described as a newly-formed talking shop.[2] Indirectly, he influenced another Scot, Sir James Frazer, for Robertson Smith became a fellow member of Trinity College, Cambridge, when he had to abandon his academic career in Scotland.

McLennan's interest in anthropology and sociology emerges in his very first publication, an article on 'Law' for the 8th edition of the *Encyclopedia* (1857).[3] Like other jurists of the time, and like the Scottish philosophers of the previous century, his intellect was engaged by the problems of the long-term development of social institutions. In the early section of this very sociological essay, McLennan deals with the growth of law and the origin of society: 'Society', he writes, 'obviously commences in the family ... the state where the government is patriarchal is indeed the direct prolongation of the family' (255–6), a proposition he was later to question. Early society deals with personal safety, property, marriage (in Anglo-Saxon the word for law is the same as that for marriage) and government. 'Government is the condition of security in the enjoyment of marriage and property' (256). This view led directly to the interest displayed in his volume on *Primitive Marriage* (1865), which carried as a sub-title, *An Inquiry into the Origin of the Form of Capture in Marriage Ceremonies.* This concern in long-term development was, of course, a recurrent one among writers of the nineteenth century, sociologists and anthropologists alike – indeed at this level there was little to distinguish these fields and McLennan refers to the work of Comte and Mill as freely as to studies of the simpler societies.

The present century saw a decline in the attention given to problems of comparison and long-term change, particularly with the increasing emphasis on fieldwork, on empirical studies, on collecting one's own data. Whether

1

these fieldworkers were studying the slums of Chicago or the islands of Melanesia, they were more concerned with the structure and function of the particular societies and institutions they were observing than with comparative or developmental analysis. For in this enterprise, considerations of long-term change often appeared to be a distraction, one indeed that might lead to a false assessment of the working of the social system; McLennan's treatment of 'marriage by capture' stands as a ghastly warning of what can go wrong, and became one of the prime examples of the evils of the comparative method in writings of the functionalist (or structural-functionalist) trend.[4] As a result of this shift, we have experienced a period marked by the diminution, often rejection, of interest in long-term, 'evolutionary' change, and of broad comparative analysis. At the same time we have seen considerable advances in the understanding of the 'other cultures', especially in the study of kinship and marriage, which minor disagreements, such as those between so-called 'descent' and 'alliance' theorists, extensionists and categorists, should not allow us to overlook.[5]

But despite the setting aside of these alternative forms of analysis, interest in this perspective has stubbornly persisted outside professional social science. Indeed even within these ranks, this interest has marked the work of those very sociologists and anthropologists that the structural and functional approaches have often taken as their models. I refer here particularly to Emile Durkheim and Max Weber, though the work of Spencer and Marx have also been used to support these types of analysis. And in anthropology one is reminded of a 'homologous' trend in the writings of that rather Durkheimian figure, Claude Lévi-Strauss, whose Saussurian commitment to the synchronic does not exclude comparison but does little to set such studies in a temporal frame, except by means of simple dichotomies or glancing references to processes such as the 'neolithic revolution'. I argue that the approach I employ is not only respectable in its forbears, general in its interest, but that it is of value even for structural or functional analyses of particular societies, as well as for the more general theory on which these studies are based. Any human institution is best understood if one can examine not only its meaning and function in a particular society but its distribution in space and time. I do not aim to substitute one approach for another, but to bring back another dimension, whose elimination from our analytic repertoire impoverishes not only the total effort towards explanation but also the individual approaches themselves, since each of these has an effect upon the others. Just as McLennan's understanding of 'marriage by capture' would have been advanced had he understood the reasons behind the institutionalised reluctance with which a new bride often goes to her husband's home (an indication among other things of the tension between wife-giver and wife-receiver, in a situation of out-marriage), so too certain problems of a structural or functional kind can be better understood in a comparative framework, which in itself implies, as Talcott Parsons has recently emphasized, an evolutionary perspective.[6]

This I have argued is true of some of the rather confused discussions about alliance and descent (J. Goody, 1973). In some cases, the perspective is already present, as in Lévi-Strauss' treatment of cross-cousin marriage and myth; but what we want is not only an interest in comparison and development, but a more rigorous and critical one.

Necessary as I believe this approach to be, the precedents are not altogether encouraging. Let us first consider the developmental picture. When the anthropology of the twentieth century has not been making strenuous efforts to avoid considering problems of long-term change, it has generally concentrated upon the evolution of systems of kin-terms, of kin groups or else of marriage, especially the marriage of cross-cousins. The first of these lines of enquiry has a long ancestry (stemming from the work of Morgan); many of the specific problems are discussed in Murdock's *Social Structure* (1949), but more recently use has been made of linguistic techniques (e.g. Dyen and Aberle, 1974). The second line, deriving from the Matrilineal and Patriarchal theories of the nineteenth century, has been treated by Gough and Aberle in their chapters in *Matrilineal Kinship* (Schneider and Gough 1961).[7] The third is pursued in Lévi-Strauss' *Elementary Structures of Kinship* (1949), where he contrasts the elementary systems of Australia, India and China with the complex structures of Africa; some of the developmental aspects of this argument have been extended and made more explicit by G. Tillion (1966).

Research of this kind has one inevitable drawback. The accounts used are mainly of recent societies, which are then placed in some overall sequence using the archaeologically-based model of progression from hunting to agriculture to industrial modes of production. If we are to draw developmental implications from our correlations, we have to accept the dangers (though not uncritically) of deriving historical inferences from cross-sectional data.[8] However a recognition of these dangers shows they are not intrinsically different, except in scale, from those arising out of the construction of developmental cycles from census data (e.g. M. Fortes' essay on 'Time and Social Structure', 1949a), or the explanation of differences in neighbouring groups by recourse to longer cycles (e.g. E. R. Leach, *Political Systems of Highland Burma*, 1954).

The examination of the long-term changes in kin-terms and descent groups has produced a somewhat limited array of results, at least in the sense that there are no very clear-cut associations. To put the point more concretely, whether 'bilateral societies' are defined by the absence of unilineal descent groups or by the presence of kinship terminologies that have no unilineal bias,[9] they are (like 'nuclear familes') seen to cluster at the top and bottom of the technological ladder, that is, among hunters and industrialists.[10] Indeed an extreme view includes both contemporary Anglo-American and pre-colonial Arctic societies under the heading of 'Eskimo social structure'.[11]

There are other correlations that provide some link with the assumed course of prehistoric events as described by archaeologists on the basis of the material evidence. Matrilineal systems, for example, are more characteristic of simple agricultural economies where farming is done with the hoe than they are of either hunting or advanced agriculture; pastoral societies are almost exclusively patrilineal. More than that, there is not a great deal to say.

Despite these difficulties, the problems raised by nineteenth-century writers are important ones. It is only by looking at the range of human societies over time and over space that we can deal with many of the kinds of question that concerned McLennan and are still unanswered today, for example, the social conditions under which monogamy or polygyny obtain. Let me take a personal example. It seemed quite natural to me as a child that of my mother's many siblings in a North Aberdeenshire township, three sisters remained unmarried throughout their lives, two living in the family house until they died. So also was the idea that they would receive a significant portion of family property, such as it was, since they had been the ones to care for my grandmother in her old age. Associated with the role of maiden aunt was the overseas migration of many males, a late age of marriage, infrequent divorce, hence little 'serial monogamy' as well as the absence of actual polygyny. These interlocking institutions, the monogamous marriage, the permanent spinster, the female inheritance of parental property, and the preferential treatment of the stay-at-home are ones we tend to regard not only as natural to our world but also (at least in many cases) as those we prefer. We make strenuous efforts (I speak collectively) to export them to other parts of the world, and we justify those preferences on grounds of rationality, discovering that they produce the most appropriate type of domestic situation for social and economic development. (Parsons, 1954; Michel, 1972).

The problem of understanding is somewhat different from what it was in McLennan's day. We are now faced with a situation where it is not simply a matter of understanding different forms of 'primitive' marriage but of understanding different forms of marriage that are practised by fellow members of the Commonwealth, of the United Nations, or of the world community. It seems to me that social anthropologists, and those of us who would prefer to describe ourselves as comparative sociologists, are running away from (or at least side-stepping) this kind of problem. We are not bringing our particular studies of human societies to bear upon some of man's central concerns, including the understanding of the long-term changes that have occurred in the field of interpersonal relations (and more specifically of kinship and of domestic institutions).[12]

Approaching these questions from a different direction, I have tried to establish some correlation between aspects of social organisation in different societies and in different parts of the world and to place these, very tentatively, in some kind of sequential ordering. Although I have had a long-standing interest in macro-evolutionary change, deriving from history and pre-history, the particular hypotheses that I tried to test arose in the first place from a detailed field study of two adjacent communities (or two sub-groups of one larger unit, it does not matter) located in northern Ghana.

In this general area every major type of descent system was found, patrilineal, matrilineal, double descent and bilateral. I was impressed by the relatively small economic differences between societies with these different systems. The bilateral systems are found in centralised states with a greater interest in trading, and often in manufacture. But the rural economies are very similar and there is little there to explain existing variations in inheritance and descent, whatever economic factors may have been involved in the origin of these different systems.

In examining the differences between these communities I gave particular attention to the mode of inheritance (the transmission of property at death) because of its effects on interpersonal relations, on kinship and affinity, especially on the relationships with the father and the mother's brother. These effects were recognised by the actors themselves and it was in following up their own explanations that I was struck by the differences between the systems of inheritance characteristic of Africa on the one hand and the major Eurasian societies on the other. It was a difference that had struck others before.

Many of the detailed observations of pre-colonial African society come from West Africa, and especially from the Gold Coast. For this region was not only the part of Black Africa closest to Europe but it was also of the greatest economic interest, especially when the Portuguese lost their monopolistic hold on the coast and the way was open for the Protestant businessmen of the western seaboard, Holland, England, Scandinavia, and north Germany, to develop the interlocking trade in gold, slaves, ivory and firearms which stood them in such stead in the early years of capital accumulation that preceded the development of industry in Europe.

During this period, at the end of the seventeenth century, the Dutch factor, William Bosman, was struck by certain features of social organisation of the Gold Coast which he saw as fundamentally different from those he had grown up with in Western Europe. Bosman was on the coast for some fourteen years and published his observations in 1705 under the title of *A New and Accurate Description of the Coast of Guinea, divided into the Gold, the Slave, and the Ivory Coasts*. In the twelfth letter of his book, the author writes 'Of the Negroes manner of Marrying'. 'Marriage here is not over-loaded with Ceremonies, nor have they any Notion of a Praevious Courtship to bring on a Match: here are no tedious Disputes on account of Marriage Settlements... The Bride brings no other Fortune than her Body, nor does the Man want much; 'tis sufficient if he has enough to defray the Expence of the Wedding-Day' (1967, 197–8). He further observes the corollary of the absence of dowry, that 'Married people here have no community of Goods; but each hath his or her particular Propriety ... On the Death of either the Man or the Wife, the respective Relations come and immediately sweep away all, not leaving the Widow or Widower the least part thereof...' (202).[13]

Thus Bosman sees that not only is conjugal community of property rare, but that a deceased's estate is not called upon to support the surviving spouse. This fact is linked to the absence of a marriage settlement, to the absence of a woman's portion of the patrimony which she brings with her into marriage as a dowry.[14] If a woman brings nothing at marriage, she gets nothing when the union is dissolved. Bosman also notes a related fact, though he does not perceive its interrelatedness. He observes that except at Accra, inheritance is matrilineal. Even in the matrilineal societies property is sex-linked ... 'the eldest Son of his Mother is Heir to his Mothers Brother or her Son, as the eldest Daughter is Heiress of her Mothers Sister or her Daughter' (203). That is to say, property descends 'homogeneously' e.g. *between* males, even when it goes *through* females.[15]

In earlier publications, I emphasised the importance of inheritance as a variable (1958, 1959, 1962) and suggested that in the domestic domain one of the major differences between African and Eurasian societies lies in the fact that in Eurasia diverging inheritance (i.e. 'bilateral' inheritance, where property goes to children of both sexes) is common, especially in the major civilisations, whereas in Africa it is virtually unknown. The absence of diverging inheritance is linked to the absence of dowry in Africa,[16] since dowry is essentially a process whereby parental property is distributed to a daughter at her marriage (i.e. *inter vivos*) rather than at the holder's death (*mortis causa*). I therefore include dowry as part of the process of 'diverging devolution'. The property a woman receives through dowry or 'bilateral' inheritance establishes some variety of a conjugal fund, the nature of which may vary widely. This fund ensures her support (or endowment) in widowhood and eventually goes to provide for her sons and daughters.

The hypothesis I evolved follows up, though not consciously, a point made by the great 'comparative sociologist' Paul Vinogradoff. He related the development of testate inheritance in Rome to systems of agriculture based upon the plough and upon the growing of grapes and olives. This form of cultivation he maintained 'did not favour either the growth of joint families or the formation of fixed holdings' but rather the development of individual property in small farms. Commenting upon this proposition in an earlier publication, I suggested that 'intensive systems of agriculture are not necessarily inconsistent with the presence of joint families or of corporate descent groups' (i.e. clans).[17]

On further reflection my comment on Vinogradoff seemed misleading. Although 'joint families' and 'unilineal descent groups' were to be found in many of the major societies of Asia, their character was qualified by the fact that part of the property attached to any such kin group was passed down to women, either in the form of the dowry at marriage or by 'bilateral inheritance' at death, i.e. through what I call 'diverging devolution'.

In examining the relationships between close kin (especially that between the mother's brother and the sister's son) I had noted that arrangements of this kind were bound to affect not only interpersonal ties[18] but the nature of the 'corporate group' as well. For under 'diverging devolution', the property which an individual disposes is not retained within the unilineal descent group of which he is a member but is distributed to children of both sexes and hence diffused outside the clan or lineage. The significance of this fact varies, of course, with the type of property involved and with the timing of its transmission.[19]

Consequently in the major Eurasian societies the kind of descent group with diverging devolution is bound to display differences from that found in African societies practising 'homogeneous inheritance', whereby a man's property is transmitted only to members of his own clan or lineage who belong to the same sex. Hence there appeared to be something wrong about comparing descent groups or ancestor worship in China and Africa (Fortes, 1961; Freedman, 1966) without fully taking into account these major variables.

Now just as the nature of the clan (and hence descent as a criterion of membership to groups) is bound to be different under these systems of inheritance, so too is marriage (and hence affinity or alliance). How does inheritance affect marriage? We have seen that in Africa, whether the system of descent is matrilineal (as among the Bemba of Zambia) or patrilineal (as among the Tallensi of Ghana), property is transmitted between members of the same sex (though not necessarily *through* them). That is to say, male property is transmitted to males and female property to females. Women are not entitled to share in the property of their fathers (or mother's brothers), even when they are members of the same unilineal descent group. The same is true of 'bilateral' (i.e. non-unilineal) societies in Africa, which have certain formal morphological similarities with kin groupings in Europe.

In the major Eurasian societies, on the other hand, women do inherit male property, despite various restrictions on the amount (half under Muslim law) and type (no land under Salic law). Alternatively they receive property not at the death of the holder but at their own marriage, in the form of dowry. The dowry may be direct or indirect; the latter is the system whereby the future son-in-law, or his family, contribute to a fund which is then settled upon the wife[20]; it is often referred to as 'brideprice' but it is a very different institution from the one existing in Africa and usually known by the same name (or, preferably, bridewealth).

In Africa the dowry occurs in societies which have been influenced by Mediterranean law, either Muslim or Christian; otherwise, where property is transferred at marriage, it takes the form of bridewealth (and in some cases, often bilateral, the absence of bridewealth) which passes between the male kin of the groom and the male kin of the bride; it has little to do with her status, except in the general sense that marriage with bridewealth is usually more prestigious than marriage without (that is, where both forms exist within a particular society).[21] The main reason appears to lie in the fact that the passage of bridewealth allocates reproductive powers over women; it is a kind of prospective childwealth.

I have tried to follow up the implications of these differences in two main ways. Firstly, I have attempted to show that there are certain 'adhesions' (to use E. B. Tylor's term) between the modes of transmitting property and other social institutions, including the mode of agricultural production and its associated technology; that is to say, I have proceeded by a form of comparative analysis. Secondly, I have tried to introduce a sequential perspective into these 'cross-sectional' studies, that is to say, I have hazarded a form of long-term developmental analysis. In testing the hypothesis, a number of correlations have been established and these have been subjected to linkage and path analysis in an attempt to test possible lines of development.

In trying to confirm the existence of this suggested difference in the distribution of forms of devolving property and their effects, we may look intensively at a selection of the major societies from the existing literature or we can make use of already coded material in the *Ethnographic Atlas* compiled under the direction of Murdock to get a wider, though less intensive, coverage. These methods may be used to supplement each other; they are not alternatives, as some over-committed scholars appear to think.

2. The theory, the variables and a test

Much work of an anthropological or sociological kind includes general statements about human societies or about the distribution of forms of marriage (e.g. monogamy or cross-cousin marriage) or types of servile institution (e.g. slavery or clientship). These statements are usually made on the basis of the one or two societies in which the individual has worked (the Trobriands or the Bororo, the Tallensi or the Kachin), together with a number of similar groups from the same region and the handful of others he currently has in memory-store. Other writers such as Spencer, Frazer, Tylor, Westermarck, Hobhouse and Ginsberg, attempted to build up more systematic procedures for the retrieval of information. More recently, the Human Relations Area Files has tried to provide a convenient store of information on a wide range of human societies. For our present purposes, the most valuable source is the *Ethnographic Atlas* (1967) which systematically codes 89 columns of information on 863 societies from all parts of the globe, enabling us to test various adhesions.

I do not use this technique in opposition to any others but to supplement other ways of examining and developing more general, more systematic and more evidence-provoking theories. Recognising all the problems that other writers have raised, often those writers who feel uncomfortable outside their particular warrens or happier dealing with broader, untestable speculations on humankind, it still seems worth while trying out such methods of testing hypotheses.

Clearly, one is limited by the coded information to testing only certain aspects of the theory, only certain aspects of its implications. For example, it could be suggested that the extent of ceremonial performed at rites of passage in the individual's life cycle is positively correlated with the amount of work (in terms of the handing over of rights and duties, etc.) that has to be done. Where marriage establishes a conjugal fund (as in dowry systems) the wedding ceremonial will be more elaborate than where it does not; where funerals redistribute the dead man's property, they will be more elaborate than where a holder divests himself of his property during his lifetime.[1]

In support of such a proposition we might cite Dumont's remark that in Hindu society, 'marriage is the most prestigious family ceremony, and at the various social levels constitutes the main occasion on which the greatest number of members of the caste and other persons gather together' (1966, 110); moreover, it is expensive and the main cause of peasant debt. With this we might contrast the great stress placed on funerals in West African society, the expenditure on which has produced protests from social reformers such as Busia (1962).

However, none of this information is coded in the present *Ethnographic Atlas* and to read through a representative sample of the relevant material would be very time-consuming. In other cases the information exists, though not always in quite the form one would wish. When it does exist, I have carried out tests of the relevant aspects of the hypothesis.[2] In so doing, I am not seeking to explain all of one 'variable' by another; in the example I gave of the relationship between life-cycle ceremonies and devolution, it is obvious that other factors are at work. The predictions are for a positive association, a significant trend, not a one to one relationship. In many branches of the social sciences a null hypothesis is rejected if the probability estimate is less than 0.05, while an association of 0.33 on a *phi* test is understood to be high (the scale runs between -1 and $+1$):[3] to this convention I will adhere in discussing the results of the tests.

There are two kinds of problem involved in carrying out such an enterprise, those to do with the instrument and those to do with the analytic concepts. From the analytic standpoint, it is the transmission of major items of property that is clearly going to be of greater significance for most relationships and institutions, especially the transmission of basic productive resources (usually land): but in the code the distinction between land and movables is made for inheritance but not for dowry. Secondly, there is a potential difficulty in deciding where property diverges. For example, a daughter may inherit her father's property in her own right or as an epiclerate, that is, a residual heir in the absence of brothers. Despite this possible ambiguity, the overall distinction is clear. In the main Eurasian societies, a close female inherited before a more distant male, even where the other male is a member of the same patrilineal descent group. In Africa south of the Sahara, a woman only inherited male property when there were no males left in the wider kingroup, and even then it was a rare occurrence.

The specific problems to do with the instrument are twofold. Firstly the compilers of the *Ethnographic Atlas* note that the inheritance data has not been easy to code; indeed they describe the code as inadequate (1967, 167). The second point has to do with marriage transactions. Since I define devolution as transmission between holder and heir (see J. Goody 1962, 312), whether or not it takes place at death, I include dowry in these operations. Indeed I include not only the 'direct dowry' (the property passed from 'parents' to a daughter on her marriage), I also include the 'indirect dowry', that is, property passed by the groom to the bride at marriage. As we have seen, such prestations are often spoken of as bridewealth or brideprice, but I would limit these terms to prestations that pass between the kin of the groom and the kin of the bride, and that can therefore be used to provide wives for the girl's brothers; in short, they form part of a system of circulating or on-going exchange. I suspect that most accounts fail to make a distinction between these types of prestation, despite the different social implications that they have. Hence what I would regard as (indirect) dowry may sometimes have been reported as brideprice.

One brief indication of the difficulties which surround the use of the term brideprice by many authors is indicated at an early date by the Ugaritic documents on marriage (Canaan, c. 1500 BC), which relate to the royal family. From these texts it is clear that 'the so-called 'bride-price' (terḫatu) is more than the conventional translation implies. It involves, certainly, the price paid by the bride-groom to the family of the bride, but it is given to the bride as a dowry' (Gray 1965, 251). The nature of the transactions involved, which I quote because they are in a sense typical of the workings of what I have called 'indirect dowry', is well illustrated by two cases recounted in the tablets. The first is that of

Ananihebi, the daughter of Ilinaru, whose terḫatu was commuted into certain property belonging to her father which became her personal property . . . The wife's terḫatu and other personal property she may possess were apparently used for the joint advantage of husband and wife during marriage, but on the death of the husband, or in case of divorce, the wife recovered her property intact, as is apparent from the case of Milka the wife of Yaṣiranu . . . This is an interesting case. Yaṣiranu is adopting a son and it is provided that, if he (Yaṣiranu) dies and his adoptive son wishes to break the association with his widow Milka, she is to receive 'the 80 shekeis of silver which she brought to Yaṣiranu' (i.e. as terḫatu) and live in her father's house (251).

As with most kinds of sociological analysis the measuring rods and the measurements themselves are bound to be less than perfect. But however crude, even such rough comparisons provide some degree of confirmation or contradiction of hypotheses about human social organisation. On the one hand this procedure gets us out of the unsystematic comparisons upon which so much comparative sociology is based and on the other hand it liberates us from certain of the limitations of the structural-functional method. It is no part of my intention to substitute one approach for another; different methods answer different problems. Indeed it is a sign of the relative immaturity of the social sciences that so many of their practitioners presume that there is a single approach to the sociological verities, an attitude which makes them more akin to politicians than to other enquirers after systematic knowledge.

Bearing in mind the limitations of this and other methods, I first looked at the distribution of diverging devolution in different continents, that is, the distribution of diverging inheritance and dowry.[4] This information was found in the following form in the *Ethnographic Atlas*:

(i) all societies where daughters have a share in either land (column 74, c, d) or movable property (76, c, d);

(ii) all societies with dowry as the main or alternative method of marriage transaction (12, d; 13, d).

The negative case consists of all those that remained once the diverging devolution data had been extracted, less those societies with no individual property rights or no rule of transmission (74, o; 76, o)[5] and those societies where there was no information on the relevant columns (74, 76, 12), i.e. any blank.

The first test was a purely distributional one, in order to confirm or refute the suggested differences between Africa and Eurasia. Table 1 shows the distribution according to the continental classification used by the *Ethnographic Atlas*. The following points emerge:

(i) In Africa, diverging devolution is rare, i.e. it occurs in 6 per cent of the cases. Bosman's observation thus has general significance.

(ii) In America, a large proportion of societies have no individual property rights or transmission rule. The reason is that, in many hunting and gathering societies, individuals had little property except personal equipment, which was often destroyed at death.[6] Inherited productive property was minimal.

(iii) In America, the relatively large number of societies with diverging

TABLE 1   *Diverging devolution by continent*

	Eurasia and Circum-Mediterranean	Africa	America	Pacific	Total
Diverging devolution:					
Present	84	12	32	32	160
Absent	75	178	58	44	355
No individual property rights or no rule of transmission	2	3	70	2	77
	161	193	160	78	592
		Total of table			592
		No information (N.I.) on devolution			271
					863

inheritance is in part a question of the importation of European norms through imperial conquest. The Mayan-speaking people of Yucatan have the same practice (Redfield, 1934, 61ff.), but I do not know whether this is an aspect of early Mayan inheritance or a European import; the people of Chan Kom, where Redfield worked, have long been Christian. Eurasian religious and secular codes (including Islam) promote diverging devolution independently of other factors.

(iv) In Eurasia and the Pacific, the societies with diverging devolution number approximately 50 per cent of the total in those areas. However, this figure includes the major civilizations, whose populations are more numerous and whose influence greater. It is suggested that the societies with homogeneous devolution are mostly those outside the major traditions, i.e. 'tribal' societies of various kinds, especially those without advanced agriculture.

Remember that the coded data is subject to a variety of errors which tend to make any positive result more significant (Köbben, 1967, 5). Moreover, an examination of the major societies in Eurasia shows an even more striking contrast. The earliest written law codes give evidence of the same kind of situation in relation to inheritance and dowry. But what other features of social organisation are associated with them? In the next three chapters, I shall neglect other forms of comparison and confine my analysis solely to the material which is available in the schedules of the *Ethnographic Atlas*, since this provides a ready-made source for comparative study. I am therefore limited in my hypotheses to what I can test by means of this coded material.

The argument continues in the following way. If women are receivers of 'male' property, either by inheritance or else by dowry, then the nature of the marriages they make will be influenced by this fact. Such influence will be particularly strong when the basic means of production, i.e. land in an agricultural society, is included in this inheritance. Where property is transmitted to women in this way, then there will be a strong tendency to control their marriages. An heiress cannot marry just anyone; her partner is more likely to have been chosen for her. Other women, too, are likely to marry (and to want to marry) within, or preferably up, rather than without and down; for unless a woman marries 'well' her status or her standard of living drops, which is often as much a matter of concern to herself as to her kinsfolk. The interest of kin takes an extreme form in the Arab injunction: 'if you cannot find an equal match, the best marriage for them is the grave' (Robertson Smith, 1907, 97). Equality, however, may involve a balance between position and wealth, for criteria of ranking are rarely single-stranded, and the rich merchant may advance his daughters by marriage to a nobler but poorer lineage, possibly even to a scholar.

If one is attempting to control marriage, it is important to control courtship too, anyhow in upper status groups where property is more significant. Choice could be controlled either by arranging a good marriage (which often involved the go-between, if it was outside one's own relatives) or by steering clear of bad ones (which might involve the chaperone).[7] In order to accomplish this end, restrictions are likely to be placed upon contact between persons of opposite sex before marriage. More particularly there will be a tendency to taboo sexual intercourse between them. For early attachments, particularly if they are likely to lead to marriage (which is essentially a jural or legal arrangement), may represent an uncontrolled element in an area of human action where control is seen as essential.

It seemed plausible to test this assumption by means of the data on premarital virginity (col. 78); a stress on virginity at marriage could be held to indicate, *inter alia*, the degree of control exercised on women by society, kin, and self. It also limits the possibility of conflicting claims on the estate in which a woman has rights. The detailed results of the test are shown in Table 2 in Appendix I; they support the idea of a positive association between societies where women inherit 'family' property and those where pre-marital sex is prohibited, the *phi* being 0.21 ($\chi^2 = 12.16, p < 0.001$).

The control of marriage itself, as distinct from courtship, is likely to take the form of encouraging homogamy – that is marriage to an individual of the same status. Indeed, in English, a marriage was frequently known as a 'match', a word that implies the pairing of like to like. This matching may be achieved by in-marriage, that is by endogamy (to use McLennan's neologism), whether this takes place within the same kindred, clan, community or caste.

The situation of endogamy is complicated by the fact that the hypothesis has to do with in-marriage in the sense of homogamy. In Europe, to some extent, the desire for like to marry like runs against the rules of the Catholic Church against marrying close kin; marriages had to take place outside the fourth degree (the rule varied somewhat in time and space). But the tendency to out-marriage among kin was counteracted by the insistence upon the 'match', upon homogamy. As Flandrin has pointed out, the Catholic Church gave both 'noble' and 'laboureur' a dispensation to marry closer kin if they could not find a partner of their own rank (1975, 37). Thus 'la règle d'homogamie' overrides 'les contraintes canoniques'. Out of 45 dispensations obtained between 1705 and 1753, in the diocese of Meaux by girls wishing to marry a kinsman, 10 made explicit reference to the need to marry a man of the same status (1975, 38).

This tendency is particularly marked where women are heirs, or even residual heirs, to property of interest to males, for they may be encouraged or obliged to marry within a certain range of kin; this was the case with the daughters of Zelophehad in ancient Israel as well as in the epiclerate of classical Athens. The *Ethnographic Atlas* does not permit us to assess the incidence of these kinds of marriage but it does enable us to get an idea of the association of one form of in-marriage, that is, endogamy (in kin, caste, or local group), with diverging devolution. The results are given in Table 3 in Appendix I ($\chi^2 = 16.09$). In it I have included all societies shown in column 19 of the Atlas (Community Organisation) as having 'a marked tendency toward local endogamy', as well as the societies in column 69 (Caste Stratification) that have either 'complex caste' or 'ethnic' stratification. I predicted that complex caste itself would be positively associated with diverging devolution. Defined 'culturally', in terms of Hindu ideology, caste is clearly limited to the Indian sub-continent. Defined 'sociologically', as a system of closed, in-marrying strata, caste is still largely confined to the Eurasian continent, or other areas where Eurasian whites have established themselves (e.g. North America, Southern Africa, the Saharan fringes).[8] Racial factors, which because of their visibility provide one of the most universal cards of identity used by man, also enter into the ban on intermarriage. But here again property is heavily involved, for there appears little reluctance for men to engage in sexual unions, as distinct from marriage, with women of the lower orders. It is the sexuality of their own sisters they are concerned to protect, and the notions regarding the purity of women that attach to caste systems and the concern with their honour that marks the Mediterranean world cannot be divorced from the position of women as carriers of property (Peristiany, 1965).

The association of complex caste[9] with diverging devolution is weak ($\chi^2 = 4.24$), the probability being < 0.05; this coefficient is acceptable but low. I do not at present offer any explanation of the low figure, except to point out the limited number of cases involved.

One form of 'homogamous' union, of the 'match', is the marriage of cousins and specifically of marriage to the father's brother's daughter (FBD) in societies with agnatic descent groups. For these cases of close marriage within the clan are often justified in terms of the retention of property or other relatively exclusive rights by near kin. It is the kind of arrangement frequently found in Arab societies, as well as in Ancient Israel, early Greece, and in traditional China, in other words in hierarchical societies where one family is likely to have significantly more or less than another, that is, to have something worth preserving by this kind of marriage.

Of course, there are societies in Africa, relatively undifferentiated, that also practise this form of marriage; the Tswana of Botswana and the Ewe of the Ghana–Togo border are cases in point. This fact raises an issue about the explanation of social institutions in general, but which applies particularly to many attempts to explain cousin marriage. In discussing social institutions (and we may take forms of preferential or prescriptive marriage as an example) we need constantly to remind ourselves that these are frequently multi-functional. Consequently any associations, 'adhesions' or correlations we discover are unlikely to be one to one. For example, I may predict that there will be an association between close in-marriage (including preferential cross-cousin marriage) and the extent of inherited property between societies, and the degree of differentiation within them; the greater the property, the closer the marriage.[10] Lévi-Strauss, on the other hand, sees cross-cousin marriage as creating ties of solidarity between social groups and as therefore specially characteristic of those simpler types of human society which have fewer alternative means of creating such ties. If we plot cross-cousin marriage against the type of economy, we do in fact find that there is a bimodal distribution such as would result from some combination of these two hypotheses. On the one hand it is frequently found in hunting and gathering societies (e.g. in Australia) and on the other it occurs in economies that have relatively advanced forms of agriculture and considerable differences in land-holding among their members (e.g. in South India). In other words, both the hypotheses could be correct because the institution (if indeed it is to be regarded as a single entity except in the vague sense of possibly having a common origin) serves diverse functions in these very different kinds of society; in any case the practice differs in respect of the explicitness of the rule and the range of kin to whom it is applied. Each hypothesis explains a certain part of the phenomena we are considering; it is not so much a matter of exceptions, much less of 'disproving' a hypothesis by one contrary example, as of discovering the conditions under which a particular theory applies.

But let us return to our main argument. Table 4 in Appendix I presents the results for father's brother's daughter marriage; there is clearly a positive association of the preferred form with diverging devolution, but if one includes the cases where it is permitted the level of association increases ($\chi^2 = 36.34$).

A system of homogamy depends of course on the recognition of the value of like marrying like and hence of avoiding marriages that involve a drop in status. But the advantages of homogamy may be more apparent to the parents than to the potential spouses, who may have their own preferences. To reinforce such a system, control has to be vested in the parental generation, a control which achieved an explicit legal status in France, under an edict of Henri II (1566). 'Que les enfants de famille ayens contracté ... mariage clandestin contre le gré et vouloir ... de leurs pères et mères ... estre ... exheretez et exclus de leurs successions.' And not only were they to be disinherited, but also subject to legal and religious sanctions (Flandrin, 1975, 42–3).

Elopement, possibly followed by a clandestine marriage, was a means by which parental will could be eluded (for Spain, see Martinez-Allier, 1974).

Elopement put pressure on the parents to accept a *mésalliance* because a married daughter was preferable to a dishonoured one. But the fact that such an escape existed led to counteraction on behalf of the state, including the insistence on the death penalty (France, 1629, see Flandrin, 1975, 44).

Since the choice of the parents could be set aside by the inclinations of girl and boy, love was potentially a rebellious passion, running contrary to reason, good sense and filial obedience. It appeared as the prelude to elopement and the clandestine marriage.

One method of reducing the likelihood of such an outcome was to try and limit contact between the sexes to authorised occasions and especially to place a high positive value on premarital virginity, for sex before marriage could diminish a girl's honour, and reduce her marriage chances (Flandrin, 1975); indeed premarital sex might also lead to a forced marriage, to an inappropriate husband.

If homogamy tends to be a feature of the major Eurasian societies, so too does monogamy. When marriage involves the matching of resources, it is difficult to duplicate the arrangement simultaneously with another wife, though there is less to inhibit additional unions of lower status, e.g. concubinage. Control over property can be exercised by the number as well as the kind of marriage. Where both males and females require parental property for the maintenance of their status, and where resources are limited, then large polygynous families are likely to have an impoverishing effect. Only the very rich can afford the luxury of many children without dropping in the economic hierarchy. In dowry systems wives might be thought of as augmenting a man's wealth and hence polygyny as a possible advantage to him; but every marriage would establish its own conjugal fund and differentiate each wife according to the marital property she brings. There are obvious difficulties for a man in setting up a plurality of such funds (though less so when the women are sisters). The test shows a positive association between diverging devolution and monogamy ($\chi^2 = 58.83$, see Appendix I, Table 5).

Like monogamy, polyandry also limits the number of wives and heirs with whom the property has to be divided and this form of marriage again displays a positive association with diverging devolution. Indeed in Tibet the provision of one legitimate heir-producing wife for a group of brothers is explicitly thought of as a way of keeping the balance between people and land (Carrasco, 1959, 36). The *Ethnographic Atlas* includes only four cases of polyandry, three of which are found in conjunction with diverging inheritance.[11]

There are two further ideas which it is possible to test with the help of the *Ethnographic Atlas*. The first has to do with residence and the second with the type of kinship terminology. As far as the first is concerned, I predicted that the inheritance of property (especially land) by women will tend to encourage alternative patterns of post-marital residence. In any society practising direct inheritance from parents to children there will be a certain number of families with no sons to take over the farm or the herd. With diverging devolution, which is a type of direct inheritance, a daughter will then become the heir, capable of attracting a husband to come and live with her. It is possible to calculate how many families will end up with only daughters as heirs or with no heirs at all, according to the varying demographic parameters. A recent survey in India showed that about 22 per cent of the families had no male heir, some 18 per cent of which will already have a daughter, and the rest no children at all. The average family size was 6.1, but it is clear that, if mortality remains constant, the proportions will be higher, the lower the average family size. With reduced mortality and reduced family size, the proportion of heirless remains high. For example, the ducal families studied by Hollingsworth (1964–5) over the period 1730–1934 had a family size of 2.8; 20 per cent of the married men had no heir. Under these conditions, the woman inheriting property (the *epicleros* of ancient Greece) is able to attract a husband to her own home rather than move to his, even where the dominant pattern of residence is virilocal. Indeed even in societies like traditional China with a strongly patrilineal ideology, the percentage of uxorilocal marriages can be high (Barclay, 1954). Hence there would seem to be a positive association between the existence of alternative residence of this kind and what I have called 'diverging devolution' or the woman's property complex. But not every woman will display these magnetic powers, which depend essentially upon the differential distribution of wealth; it is only the rich or epicleratic daughter who finds herself in such a position. So that we should not expect a straightforward uxorilocal pattern of post-marital residence but rather an ambilocal one, where a married couple may choose to reside with the kin of either the bride or the groom depending upon their relative position. There is another possibility: if an independent conjugal fund is established at marriage, bride and groom may also establish an independent (i.e. neolocal) residence.[12]

The results of this test are shown in Table 6 in Appendix I, where $\chi^2 = 26.90$. However, the overall figures conceal part of the problem, and a further breakdown is given in Table 7. From this Table it will be seen that, while bilocal and neolocal marriage are definitely correlated with diverging devolution, the correlation is negative where the alternative forms of marriage represent less than one-third of the total (Pu, Pm, Vu, Vm in the code). The latter finding is contrary to my hypothesis. However, the determinants of residence are not of course limited to property. Indeed in this instance it seemed possible that the absence of unilineal descent groups (i.e. 'bilateral descent') would prove to have a close association with the pattern of residence. In Table 7 diverging devolution and bilateral kinship are compared in terms of their association with types of residence.

I return to this question later when I compare 'bilaterality' and 'diverging devolution' as variables. Here I want to point out that it is only in respect of residence that kinship is as good a predictor as the transmission of property. Part of the answer emerges from a study of the figures for the residence patterns of societies that have 'no individual property rights or no regular rules of transmission'. The interesting point about Table 7 is the vary large proportion of these societies that include marriages of the 'bilocal' or 'virilocal with alternatives' types – no doubt because there is no immovable property to tie anyone anywhere.

Let me next turn to that favourite anthropological topic, kinship terminologies. The terms for kinsfolk of one's own generation used in English (of a type curiously known as 'Eskimo') tend to isolate the children of siblings from one another. There are other types of terminology that do this, apart from Eskimo; in essence these systems separate the children of a conjugal pair from the children of their siblings. In a society that practices direct inheritance, that is, transmission from parents to children, and at the same time cuts siblings off from one another at marriage by establishing separate conjugal funds on their behalf, this isolating situation would tend to be reflected in a kinship terminology that differentiates siblings from cousins. And indeed we find in Table 8 (Appendix I) that this hypothesis is also supported by the *Ethnographic Atlas*, the χ^2 for the correlation with diverging devolution being 31.65. In other words, the isolation of the nuclear family (in this particular form and in this particular sense) is nothing new; it did not come with the industrial revolution but is a function of direct inheritance.

The thesis I am putting forward here to do with 'sibling kinship terms' is similar to that discussed by Dole (1965) and based upon the hypothesis of L. H. Morgan that the accumulation of property and its inheritance by individuals (i.e. direct inheritance) were crucial in the development of 'descriptive' (i.e. individualising) nomenclatures for kin rather than classificatory ones.

There is one powerful motive which might, under certain circumstances, tends [sic.] to the overthrow of the classificatory form and the substitution of the descriptive ... This is the inheritance of estates ... The rights of property ... would be adequate beyond any other known cause to effect a radical change in a pre-existing system ... In Tamilian society, where my brother's sons and my cousin's sons are both my sons, a useful purpose may have been subserved by drawing closer, in this manner, the kindred bond; but in a civilized sense it would be manifestly unjust to place either of these collateral sons upon an equality with my own son for the inheritance of my estate. Hence the growth of property and the settlement of its distribution might be expected to lead to a more precise discrimination of the several degrees of consanguinity if they were confounded by the previous system (Morgan, 1871, 14).

All these variables I am discussing are interrelated in a field with reciprocal effects on one another. But I see diverging devolution (especially dowry) as the main mechanism by which familial status was maintained in an economically differentiated society, and which in turn has important implications for kinship and marriage. But while I have used inheritance, or rather devolution, as the independent (or exogenous) variable, it is independent only in a certain context. For these hypotheses raise a further series of questions concerning the factors behind diverging devolution itself. Why should the African and Eurasian patterns be so different? I suggest that the scarcer productive resources become and the more intensively they are used, then the greater the tendency towards the retention of these resources within the basic productive and reproductive unit, which in the large majority of cases is the nuclear family. There are several reasons for this hypothesis. Advanced agriculture, whether by plough or irrigation, permits an individual to produce much more than he can consume. Given sufficient incentives and adequate distribution, the greater volume of production can maintain an elaborate division of labour and a stratification based upon different 'styles of life'. An important means of maintaining one's style of life, and that of one's progeny, is by marriage with persons of the same or higher qualifications.[13] We should therefore expect a greater emphasis upon the direct vertical transmission of property in societies with advanced rather than simple exploitation of agricultural resources. This system of direct vertical transmission (i.e. from parents to children) tends to make provision for women as well as men. The position of women in the world has to be maintained by means of property, either in dowry or inheritance – otherwise the honour of the family suffers a setback in the eyes of itself and others. This also means that women are likely to become residual heirs in the restricted sibling groups that monogamy permits, the property going to female descendants before collateral males, even when these are members of the same agnatic clan.

The other aspect of advanced agriculture bearing upon the conditions for the emergence of diverging devolution is the expansion of population it allows, another factor making for scarcity of land. Where such agriculture is dependent upon the plough, the increase in production is partly a result of the greater area a man can cultivate; once again, land becomes more valuable, especially the kind of land that can sustain permanent cultivation by means of the simpler type of plough.

Intensive exploitation of resources can be variously assessed. The *Ethnographic Atlas* demonstrates the firm association that exists between the presence of the plough and diverging devolution (Appendix I, Table 9). The information on plough agriculture is not altogether satisfactory since the absence of an entry in column 39 might mean either no information or no plough; however the presence of the plough is such an obvious feature of human cultures that the chance of error should be small. The Atlas also gives a separate code for intensive agriculture (col. 28 I, J), which is somewhat less strongly associated. Advanced agriculture is virtually a condition of the extensive differentiation by styles of life that in turn encourages the concentration of property by inheritance and marriage. This concentration is maintained by diverging devolution, which takes the form of direct vertical transmission; hence the importance of 'sonship', real and fictional (which includes daughters), in these areas of social action.[14] We would therefore expect to find diverging devolution associated with complex stratified societies of all types, whether characterised by caste or class. This hypothesis (tested in Table 11, Appendix I) is linked to the suggestion that diverging devolution encourages endogamy (Table 3, Appendix I). Endogamy is clearly one way of limiting the consequences of the transmission of property through women. Other systems of complex stratification may restrict marriage *de facto* if not *de jure*.

The association of diverging devolution with a relatively advanced economy also suggests a link with the more complex political systems. Column 33 provides 'a measure of political complexity', from which I have selected only the larger states. In surveying the major Eurasian civilisations, all (in differing degrees) were found to be characterised by diverging devolution; women were usually residual heiresses to their brothers, in addition to which they received a dowry if they married away. These forms of marriage prestation and inheritance are recorded in the Greek, Roman, the Hebrew and Chinese texts and in Babylonian, Hindu, and Buddhist law-books. For such societies were all literate; indeed testamentary inheritance, as Maine pointed out, was sometimes used to divert property from a man's agnates, who were his residual heirs. But more often and more universally the institution of adoption (often of agnates) and the 'appointed daughter' were used to ensure the direct vertical transmission of property. In general, these literate societies fall into the category of 'large states' (or are closely linked to them) and the association with diverging devolution is shown to be firm (Appendix I, Table 12).

Tylor long ago pointed out the adaptive functions of exogamy for human societies (1889). Mankind, he remarked, was faced with the alternative of marrying out or being killed out. In-marriage on the other hand is a policy of isolation. One reason among others for such a policy is to preserve property where this is transmitted through both males and females, to encourage marriages with families 'of one's own kind' and thus to maintain property and prestige. The positive control of marriage arrangements (exogamy is a negative control) is stricter where property is transmitted to women. It is a commentary on their lot that where they are more propertied they are initially less free as far as marital arrangements go, though the unions into which they enter are more likely to be monogamous (or even polyandrous).

In this chapter I have tried to use the *Ethnographic Atlas* to test a set of hypotheses to do with the concomitants of diverging devolution, derived from a more intensive study of the literature on a number of societies in Eurasia and Africa. Though the information is imperfect and the instrument limited, the basic suggestions are all confirmed (except in the case of caste). Eurasian and African societies differ in their systems of transmitting property; these differences are correlated with differences in the types of marriage prestation, the extent of control over women, both before marriage and in terms of marriage partners (and probably after marriage too, though this I could not test in the same way). Differences in the nature of a man's estate are indicated in the greater prevalence of kin terms that isolate the sibling group, an indication of the differences in the type of descent corporation found associated with the different ways of devolving property and the different modes of agriculture. Both the means and the relations of production display a number of marked differences.

It is a failure to recognise these differences in the type of descent corporation (even when both can be described, for example, as 'patrilineal descent groups') that seems to have caused much of the controversy over the application of descent or alliance models to the study of these societies and it is significant that so-called 'descent theorists' have generally worked with systems of homogeneous devolution and the 'alliance theorists' with systems of diverging devolution.[15] It should be apparent that where marriage involves a re-arrangement of property rights of the dowry kind, then conjugal, affinal, sibling, and filial relationships are likely to display qualitative differences from systems of the African kind. It also follows that the organisation of descent groups will differ under these two conditions. The ball-play between rival 'theorists' has obscured the basic differences in the material they are dealing with.

I conclude by pointing to the association of diverging transmission with intensive (and plough) agriculture, with large states and with complex systems of stratification. In such societies social differentiation based on productive property exists even at the village level; to maintain the position of the family, a man endows (and controls) his daughters as well as sons, and these ends are promoted by the tendency towards monogamous marriage. Indeed it is significant that of the variables originally considered, the strongest associations of diverging devolution are with monogamy and plough agriculture. But relatively advanced politico-economic systems that are represented by the four variables above seem more likely to lead to diverging devolution than to stem from it and it is this suggestion we shall try and explore in the next chapter.

3. Making causal inferences

Having looked at the relationship between kinship and property (a central theme in McLennan's writing), we come back to Vinogradoff's concern with agriculture and the economy. Diverging devolution is the transmission of property to children of both sexes. It arises, I suggest, when parents are concerned to maintain the status of their children *vis-à-vis* other members of the community, and particularly the status of their daughters, by means of the settlement of property. Hence it is likely to appear in societies in which status is based on economic differentiation. Indeed it is both a cause and effect of a certain type of stratification. When differences of economic status emerge, when one wants to control the marriages of daughters or sisters in terms of that status, then dowry is the characteristic marriage transaction.[1]

There are many ways in which this degree of economic stratification may arise, but in the present context the critical one is by means of an increase in productivity that permits and encourages greater differentiation than is possible under, say, the conditions of hoe farming. The work of Gordon Childe on the prehistory of the Middle East, as well as that of McNeill in the wider context of world history, suggests that the most important way of increasing production is by mechanising agricultural production, as when animal traction is used to plough the land. Childe (1954a, 73) saw that the limitations of the first agricultural economies lay in their self-sufficiency and in their consequent inability to build up a social surplus which would allow of specialisation: 'the expansion in numbers involved expansion in space', he declared, not the division of labour. The contradictions inherent in these simple productive systems were transcended only when farmers 'were persuaded or compelled to wring from the soil a surplus above their own domestic requirements, and when this surplus was made available to support new economic classes not directly engaged in producing their own food' (77). The realisation of this surplus rested upon a number of basic inventions: irrigation agriculture, metallurgy, the wheel, the sailing ship, animal power, writing and the plough; these discoveries 'provided the foundations for a new economic organization' (97). But above all 'the revolutionary solution [to the pressure of population on land] was to intensify the exploitation of the existing land, and to use the regular surplus thereby extracted for the support of full-time specialists who did not produce their own food' (1954b, 45). It was this intensive agriculture that produced a radical change 'in social structure and psychology, as well as in economy'. The technological and economic changes in the system of production and distribution were prerequisites of what Childe called the urban revolution that occurred in the temple cities of Uruk and elsewhere in Mesopotamia; an elaborate bureaucracy, a complex division of labour, a stratified society based on ecclesiastical landlordism, all this was made possible by intensive agriculture where title to landed property was of supreme importance (Mallowan, 1965, 14).

Since Childe wrote, new archaeological evidence has thrown more light upon the considerable cultural achievements of the earlier agricultural societies of the Middle East, of the Palestine—Jordan region (as typified by Jericho), of southern Anatolia (especially Çatal Hüyük) and of the Zagros mountains. Already in Çatal Hüyük there is evidence of craft specialisation and internal stratification. Even at this stage, these developments in the social order rest on the basis of what Mellaart (1967) describes as 'intensive agriculture'. And the yet earlier settlement of Jericho gives some evidence of the use of irrigation (Mellaart, 1961, 57). In Iran, the other major area of early agricultural development, the crucial advances towards population expansion and urban life took place somewhat later, in the period 5500—4000 B.C., 'the era of early irrigation farming and cattle domestication' (Hole and Flannery, 1967, 181). 'The increasing division of labour, which had made food production an efficient and dependable means of subsistence, produced storable surpluses ("wealth") which could be used to support further division of labour in the way of craft activities' (201). Two thousand years later, more sophisticated irrigation and the cultivation of improved cereals, with the cattle-drawn plough 'carried some peoples in south-western Iran to the threshold of civilization' (181).

With the introduction of irrigation 'fields became improved property on which labour had to be spent regularly' (202). They were recipients of a major investment of capital. Cattle, also introduced during the sixth millennium, were harnessed to the plough in the third, 'thus greatly increasing the amount of land a single man could put under cultivation' (202). In some areas the centripetal forces acting upon village size were reduced, a change that allowed the build-up of towns, of larger, denser, more differentiated residential aggregates.

The role of intensive agriculture, by plough or by irrigation, is seen as critical in the developments that occurred after 2000 B.C., developments that we suggest produced (or encouraged) the diverging devolution of property that was recorded in Babylonian laws not very long after the period to which we refer (Driver and Miles, 1952).

While such developments in the sphere of 'family law' were not limited to areas of intensive exploitation of land or livestock (they were spread, for example, by military conquest and by religious conversion), it is significant that they did not occur in Africa until the advent of religious systems from the Middle East. Cattle and cereals are found in many parts of Africa; but the third crucial innovation of the period prior to 4000 B.C., that is, irrigation, did not spread south of the Nile valley. Neither, of course, did the more sophisticated irrigation techniques and the cattle-drawn plough of the later period. The reasons do not concern us here – only the implications of the failure to introduce these critical advances. But it should be said that some authors attribute the persistence of shifting cultivation in Africa to the poor quality of the soils (Allan, 1965, 3); Lord Hailey once remarked that 'shifting cultivation is less a device of barbarism than a concession to the character of the soil'. Others have seen the men as reluctant to take on the additional burden of plough agriculture, especially as women generally play a larger part in shifting cultivation (Boserup, 1970, 33). However this may be, the change in productive system will clearly have an important effect on social organisation.

By this means a man's potential area of cultivation during one season could be increased from about 6 acres to a theoretical possibility of some 60 acres.[2] The implications of this great change for interpersonal relations have not been fully understood. For differentiation arose even at village level and the scene was set for the development of relationships such as lord and serf, landlord and tenant, which exist in Eurasia but not in Africa. These differences are ones which are likely to affect the strategy of marriage, encouraging a move from exogamy to endogamy, from out-marriage to in-marriage, in an attempt to preserve the status of one's offspring.

We can now introduce a vectorial factor in the study of kinship systems, albeit crudely. We have a network of interrelated hypotheses, a theory for the development of kinship systems. As distinct from many attempts to correlate unilineal descent groups or the nuclear family with the economy, here we can see reasoned associations between changes in the productive system and the changes in kinship institutions. But how can we try and test the causal implications?

In thinking of the relationship between human institutions, we constantly speak in vaguely causal terms. We discuss various *causes* of the French Revolution, or maintain that the Protestant ethic was *the crucial factor* in the development of capitalism; or see divorce rates as *depending* upon the strength of the sibling bond; or matrilateral cross-cousing marriage as *implying* certain structural arrangements. In all these cases we not only recognise an association between two or more factors but we also impute, however tentatively, a vectorial element, a direction.

Comparative sociology (in which we include social anthropology) has, however, had little time for causal analysis. Partly this aversion has been the result of the kind of data with which it is dealing, and the kinds of method which it is able to use; here the absence of diachronic data and of the experimental method are of critical importance. But Radcliffe-Brown (1957, 42) has also argued that relationships can be analysed more accurately in terms of co-variation rather than cause, since 'it is the system as a whole which is involved in cause'. This approach, which displays the holistic bias of functional and structural writers, smacks too much of making a virtue out of a necessity; we still continue to think and act in causal terms, which can be dropped from the social sciences only to their detriment, though the appropriate place for their introduction must always be a matter of assessment.

In the social sciences the problem of cause is twofold. It is not simply a matter of establishing direction but of weighting the different factors. Arguments which centre upon dismissing one cause, or type of causes, in order to establish another (e.g. social versus biological) are of limited usefulness; we need to know the relative influence of a variety of factors on a particular situation; or, alternatively, we need to examine a variety of consequences of a particular factor. The problem is not one of rejection or acceptance but of measurement and judgement.

The other main problem is one of proof. Hypotheses that claim to account for a large set of data are not hard to come by; it is selecting from among the alternatives that is a major stumbling block. Do we have to choose on the basis of fashion? Or are there other ways of sifting the proposed theories?

The problem is one that was faced, in a different context, by Marc Bloch, a scholar who successfully combined the techniques of the field worker with historical, sociological and comparative studies. In the volume in which he offers a summary of the history of rural France, he shows how the distribution of agrarian systems was linked to the use of the Mediterranean and Germanic ploughs, the *aratrum* and the *charrue*. He is tempted by his argument 'to trace the whole chain of causation back to a single technological innovation. The wheeled plough produced long-furlong fields; long-furlong fields provided a powerful and constant incentive to collective practice, and hey presto, a set of wheels fixed to a plough-share becomes the basis of an entire social structure' (Bloch, 1966, 54–5). But Bloch is more careful: the necessity for collective discipline in the practice of regular crop rotation and of common grazing suggests that the argument could be reversed and that without communal habits of cultivation the wheeled plough could never have been adopted. He goes on to comment:

There are obviously inherent difficulties in attempting to make such exact appraisals of cause and effect for a development whose course can only be plotted by guess-work. So let us content ourselves with a less ambitious observation: for as far back in time as we can go, the wheeled plough (parent of the long-furlong field) and a collective habit of cultivation are the twin characteristics of one very distinct type of agrarian civilisation; where these criteria are lacking the civilization will be of a totally different type.

We are entitled to be more ambitious as our techniques improve. The previous discussion concerning the relationship between advanced agriculture and diverging devolution presumed a causal or at least a temporal chain, but it only tried to demonstrate correlation. In this chapter, we attempt to seek out the causal implications of these correlations by using two techniques which are becoming increasingly important in the social sciences, namely linkage and path analysis. These techniques have usually been applied to more rigorously collected data than we have at our disposal. We recognise the limitations of this material, but it has seemed worth while experimenting with these techniques as a method of exploring their possible uses. We were encouraged in this not only by the work of Blalock, but also, after the publication of our original paper (J. Goody *et al.* 1971), by the support of Hadden and DeWalt who gave further examples of the use of path analysis (1974). Because discussions of this technique are easily available in print, I shall simply summarize the results.

In the original publication, the variables used were those we have already described. We first established a matrix of correlations of each variable against each other. The next step was to subject the matrix to a hierarchical linkage analysis, which is essentially a clustering device (McQuitty, 1960; see Goody *et al.*, 1971, for other references) which groups pairs of variables on the basis of the highest reciprocal correlation. The result of these operations based upon the tables in Appendix I are shown in Figure 1; they can be used to help build the theoretical model which is to be tested by means of path analysis.

We tested a number of such models but the one that gave the best all round fit was that presented in Figure 2. Here the values lay within 0.001 and 0.002, which gave a very good approximation. Moreover, we earlier repeated these procedures on a number of other samples of societies listed in the *Ethnographic Atlas*, including ones suggested by Naroll and Murdock as ways of getting round 'Galton's problem', the problem of diffusion. All give slightly different sets of correlations, which seem to reflect differences in continental distribution (Buckley and Goody, 1974). But in the large majority of cases, the model suggested in Figure 2 provided the best fit.

This was still true when we combined certain of the original variables. For general reasons, and because there might be some overlap, it seemed best to combine 'endogamy' and 'father's brother's daughter marriage' into a composite variable called 'in-marriage'; to combine 'plough agriculture' and 'intensive agriculture' to form 'advanced agriculture'; and to put 'large states' with 'stratification' to make up 'complex polity'. The details of the correlations of these variables with diverging devolution (*phi* = 0.32, 0.22 and

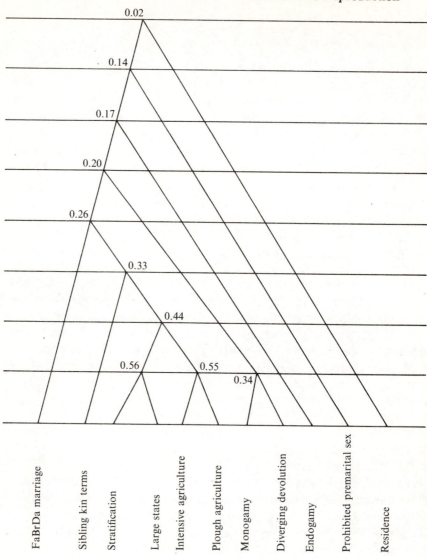

FIGURE I   Hierarchical linkage of the devolution variables

0.25 respectively) are given in Tables 13, 14 and 15 in Appendix I. I should
add that, as with the previous tables these have all been recalculated to take
into account additions and corrections to the *Ethnographic Atlas* since 1967,
whereas the calculations in the original papers were made on the basis of

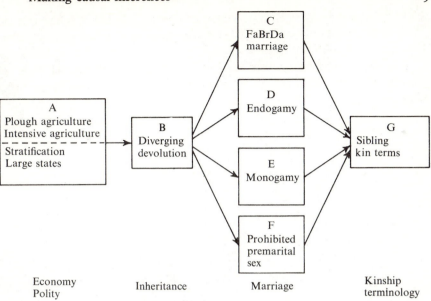

FIGURE 2   Causal model for path analysis

the slightly different figures then available. The reason for not redoing these calculations in the same form has to do with developments in the analysis; it seemed preferable to utilise the more recent techniques by A.I.D. (Automatic Interaction Detector) analysis described by Sonquist, Baker and Morgan in *Searching for Structure* (1973; see also Sonquist and Morgan, 1964), which attempts to make greater use of the computer to seek out the effects of interaction between variables. But, as far as our original calculations were concerned, they should be little affected by the minor changes that were made.

While our model is plausible in terms of theoretical and mathematical constraints, it is certainly not the only possible outcome. Although we tried as many alternatives as we could, limitations of time and energy inhibited us from testing every possibility. Moreover, the model is incomplete; variables not given in the *Ethnographic Atlas* are by definition excluded. But even some variables listed in the Atlas were not originally used by us when they would have been appropriate. In the original discussion, I tried to see whether some other variable could be substituted for 'diverging devolution' to give equally good results. I tried 'bilateral kinship' since the kind of transmission in which I am interested is sometimes called 'bilateral'. However the correlations were generally much weaker, largely I suspect because 'bilateral kinship' is found in a whole variety of contexts, being essentially a situation deriving from the absence of unilineal descent groups.

The more important omission, namely, the economic role of men and women, was later included in our analysis and is the subject of the following chapter.

4. Farming, labour and sex

The relationship between these broad aspects of human societies, linking certain facets of the economic, political and kinship systems, has received some support in a study emanating from a different quarter and using different sources. This is Ester Boserup's work, *The Role of Women in Economic Development* (1970) which examines national and regional data collected from U.N., governmental and other agencies. A second study, by Germaine Tillion, and entitled *Le Harem et les cousins* (1966) is more impressionistic, being based upon the author's own fieldwork among the Berber and her wider acquaintance with the Mediterranean area. A central concern of both authors is the role of women under different socio-economic conditions.

The distinction between systems with diverging devolution and those with homogeneous transmission corresponds in some respect to that between the presence of dowry and bridewealth, or, to put the matter more precisely, the presence of each of these forms of marital transaction is consistent with their counterparts at the level of inheritance. It is also consistent with the distinction between endogamic and exogamic systems of marriage to which Germaine Tillion called attention (Tillion, 1966; Michel, 1972).

Tillion contrasts the exogamic nature of 'savage' society, characterised by populations of low density, scattered throughout the world at some distance from each other and now in the process of disappearing, with the prolific endogamous societies distributed around the borders of the Mediterranean. By 'savage', she means essentially hunting and gathering societies where daughters are used to make alliances with neighbours to guarantee the respective territories. Hence the ban on marrying relatives (exogamy), to which the incest prohibition, out-marriage and monogamy, are seen as related. Such societies, she claims, require to balance resources against population and hence exercise a policy of demographic control. These elementary or primary structures are opposed to the secondary or endogamic structures which, based upon a new agricultural economy, encouraged a population explosion. These conditions released societies from the obligation of creating alliances and they turned instead to marriages within rather than without. This 'sociologie néolithique', she claims, is marked by the prohibition on

31

exchange, the return to 'incest', polygyny, war and racism, slavery, patrilineal filiation, female virginity, and demographic expansion.

The work of Tillion takes its departure from Lévi-Strauss' dichotomy
between elementary and complex systems of kinship and marriage, a dichotomy which she properly wishes to complicate. But her thesis suffers from its
lack of sustained argument and more particularly of systematic testing; the
assumptions concerning population could have easily been tested and would
have been shown to be false. The work of Ester Boserup, on the other
hand, does attempt to bring data to bear upon theory in a more systematic
way.

In looking at the background to the role of women in development,
Boserup distinguishes between 'male and female farming systems' (1970),
which she then tries to relate to population density, technology and type of
cultivation. Her thesis is summarised in the following words: 'in very sparsely
populated regions where shifting cultivation is used, men do little farm work,
the women doing most. In somewhat more densely populated regions where
the agricultural system is that of extensive plough cultivation, women
do little farm work and men do much more. Finally, in the regions of intensive
cultivation or irrigated land, both men and women must put hard work into
agriculture in order to earn enough to support a family on a small piece of
land' (1970, 35).

She associates the sexual division of labour with differences in the position
of women in rural communities which fall into two broad groups:

the first type is found in regions where shifting cultivation predominates and the major part of
agricultural work is done by women. In such communities, we can expect to find a high incidence of polygamy [polygyny], and bride wealth being paid by the future husband or his
family. The women are hard-working and have only a limited right of support from their
husbands, but they often enjoy considerable freedom of movement and some economic
independence from the sale of their own crops.
The second group is found where plough cultivation predominates and where women
do less agricultural work than men. In such communities we may expect to find that only a
tiny minority of marriages, if any, are polygamous; that a dowry is usually paid by the girl's
family; that a wife is entirely dependent upon her husband for economic support; and that
the husband has an obligation to support his wife and children, at least as long as the marriage
is in force (50).

This thesis has much in common with that which we have developed in our
earlier studies attempting to relate types of production and aspects of kinship
and marriage. There we tried to link patterns of transmitting property to forms
of agriculture ('shifting' against 'advanced') and polity as the 'independent'
variables, and forms of marriage, kinship terminologies, etc., as the 'dependent'
ones. How does the sexual division of labour relate to these earlier variables?
Clearly, if diverging devolution is connected with plough agriculture, then

following Boserup's hypothesis, it should also be connected with a male predominance in agricultural activities. Since the *Ethnographic Atlas* codes information on the roles of the sexes in farming, we can test the strength of the relationship to the prevailing type of agriculture (Table 16, Appendix I). Leaving aside the cases of equal participation, the difference between male and female farming is marked, male farming being associated with the more advanced agriculture while female farming is found mainly with simple agriculture ($\chi^2 = 77.53$). As predicted by Boserup the association is strong.

A further variable discussed by Boserup is that of population density. We cannot test this directly, as the information is not included in the *Ethnographic Atlas*. The nearest indicator, not a very satisfactory one, is the size of the local community (Table 17, Appendix I). Here we find that societies with male farming tend to have larger communities than where female labour predominates; 59 per cent of those with male farming fall into the 400 plus category and most of these are over 10,000; in contrast only 22 per cent of those with female farming have communities of 400 and over and few of these are over 10,000. Thus some support is given to the idea of greater population density in societies with male farming as opposed to those with female farming. On the other hand, according to Boserup's argument, equal participation ought to be more closely associated with 'intensive' as distinct from plough agriculture and with communities of the largest size. However, this form of the division of labour between the sexes is found in a wide range of societies, including those where agriculture no longer plays the dominant role in the economy.

Boserup argues that the contrast between shifting cultivation with female farming and plough cultivation with male farming, where women are either secluded in the home or occupied almost wholly in the domestic sphere, is also related to 'the difference in the pattern of social hierarchy between regions of tribal organization and regions of settled farmers with individual ownership of land' (27). Plough agriculture is found in areas where there is private land ownership and a landless class whose labour is available for hire. 'As hired labourers are called in, so are the women of cultivator families released from agricultural work. On the other hand, women always seem to bear a large part of the work burden in the more egalitarian communities' (31). When we test the association between the sexual division of labour and complex polity we find that the correlation between female agriculture and the simple type of polity is strong ($\chi^2 = 28.6$); as with dowry, male farming is positively linked to the more complex polities.

The role of women in agriculture is also seen as connected with the type of marriage. In regions of female farming, Boserup writes, women are valued both as workers and as child bearers; in 'such communities, we can expect to find a high incidence of polygamy, and bride wealth being paid by the future husband or his family' (50). On the other hand, where women do little agricultural work, they are valued as mothers only and the status of a barren woman is particularly vulnerable; in such communities 'we may expect to find that only a tiny minority of marriages, if any, are polygamous; that a dowry is usually paid by the girl's family' (50). This proposition is very closely related to our discussion of the role of dowry and bilateral inheritance in channelling property to daughters. The distribution of sex roles in agriculture in relation to the plurality of marriage is shown in Table 18 (Appendix I). Monogamy is most likely to be found with male farming and general polygyny the least likely (though limited polygyny is common); the reverse occurs with female farming.[1]

With marriage transactions, shown in Table 19, the position is less clear; male farming is somewhat less strongly associated with bridewealth than is female farming (or equal participation) and slightly more so with dowry, though the number of cases of the latter is small. However dowry, as we have seen, is part of a more widespread system of intergenerational transmission we have called 'diverging devolution', which includes inheritance by women as well as transmission at marriage. The association of male farming with this wider variable turns out to be strong ($\chi^2 = 46.35$), stronger indeed than the other associations we established in the first chapter.

When we compare the correlations of these two variables, i.e. devolution and division of labour by sex, we find that in two cases diverging devolution produces the best results, in four cases the division of labour does (Table 20). When we examine the individual results, we find that the division of labour behaves better in relation to the two 'independent' variables, namely 'advanced agriculture', and 'complex polity'. This is to be expected.

TABLE 20   *Diverging devolution and division of labour: phi coefficients compared*

	(1) Diverging devolution	(2) Male farming	(3) Prohibited premarital sex	(4) Sibling kin terms	(5) Advanced agriculture	(6) Complex polity	(7) In-marriage	(8) Monogamy
Diverging devolution	—	0.40	0.21	0.28	0.22	0.25	0.32	0.34
Division of labour	0.40	—	0.19	0.29	0.42	0.26	0.33	0.26

The sexual division of labour in farming is bound to be closely linked to the type of agriculture, the relations of production to the means of production. In particular the plough is an instrument employed almost entirely by men; indeed it is the case that all large livestock, whether horses, cattle or camels, are almost exclusively in male hands. Their use in advanced agricultural production means that the male role becomes if not dominant, then at least equal to that of women, who frequently play the major productive roles in hoe farming.

This can be seen from the distribution of female farming shown in the Ethnographic Atlas, which resembles the distribution of systems of devolution (Table 21, Appendix I). Plough agriculture with male farming is largely confined to Eurasia; in Africa, hoe farming with female farming predominates; in North America, although most societies have hunting economies, female farming is associated with extensive, male farming with intensive agriculture. In the Pacific, the predominant horticulture is not exclusively associated with any type of division of labour by sex, though equal participation is only slightly less frequent than in Eurasia.

The introduction of a new factor, the division of labour by sex, necessitates the construction of a new model to be tested by linkage and path analysis. The linkage analysis, based upon the matrix of correlation coefficients presented in Table 22 (Appendix I), gives a rather similar picture to that presented in the previous chapter (Figure 1, p. 28).[2] Figure 3 shows a close linkage, at the first level, between advanced agriculture and division of labour (A), and a slightly less close link between diverging devolution and monogamy (B). At the second level, complex polity is linked to the sexual division of labour and advanced agriculture (A above) almost as closely as the latter to themselves; in-marriage is linked in a similar way to diverging devolution and monogamy (B). At the third level, sibling kin terms are associated with the polity—economy pairing (A above), and at the fourth all these above variables are clustered together leaving only prohibited premartial sex at the fifth level. There are three versions of an alternative procedure, the Median, the Minimum (also known as the 'nearest neighbour' method which links clusters by the highest correlation within them) and finally the Maximum method, which links clusters by the lowest correlation within them, and hence imposes more stringent conditions. Figure 3 is based upon the Median method and is similar in shape to that produced by applying the McQuitty techniques, except that the values are a little different. The most rigorous of the alternative methods gives a slightly different picture in that complex polity joins in-marriage at level 1 before being linked with the economic variables at level 3. In these hierarchies the sexual division of labour is closer to the political and economic variables (as one might expect) than to diverging devolution, which approaches more closely

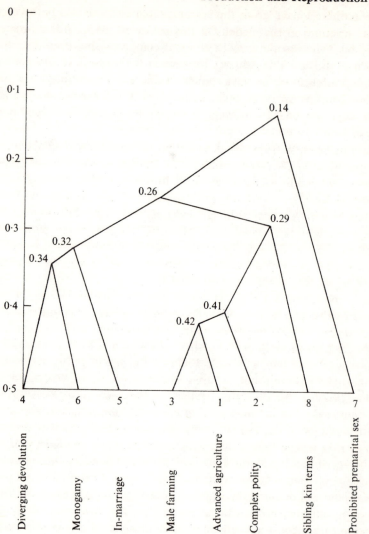

FIGURE 3 Hierarchical linkage of the revised devolution variables and the sexual division of labour

the 'kinship' variables with the one exception of the kin terminology, which is linked more directly to the major 'independent' variables concerned with the economy and the polity.

The causal model suggested in the previous chapter was revised to take account of the added variable and the new linkage analysis; it is presented in

Figure 4 where I have given the economic (agriculture) and polity variables separate positions in the model. On this subject R. McC. Adams writes that 'Almost by definition the growth of social complexity has been accompanied by social stratification' (1966, 79). He goes on to discuss L. H. Morgan's thesis on the development of the state and concludes, 'most students would shift the emphasis from property as such, socially defined and maintained rights to certain resources or commodities, to the system of stratified social relations of which rights to property were only an expression' (1966, 80). However, in most (though not all) contexts, I would see the system of production and the related system of land tenure or property holding as a prior variable to class or state, though the legal definition of property would clearly require the existence of a state.

Any model of this kind is inevitably a gross over-simplification of reality; in order to apply path analysis it is necessary to assume a one-way flow, a separation of variables, relative to one another, into dependent and independent. Moreover, in this particular instance it was also necessary to impose a strict ordering on the variables, an order that is indicated by the numbers on the model as it emerges from the numerical test (Figure 5). Once again this test was carried out by J. C. Mitchell, who comments 'From this model you will see that a great deal of your paradigm survives quite well.'[3]

There are other aspects of Boserup's thesis that could be pursued. The connection between female farming and matriliny has been the subject of much discussion from Hahn (1896) and Baumann (1928) to Schneider and Gough (1961).[4] There is the associated problem of the house-property complex, an institution that exists in many parts of Africa and one by which male property is distributed by stocks (i.e. by mothers) rather than by heads (Gluckman, 1950; Goody and Buckley, 1972). It raises the question of the relationship of polygyny to hoe agriculture, as well as the distribution of purdah and the withdrawal of women from 'economic' life. Indeed it raises in acute form the whole problem of defining the woman's contribution to the economy. But here I have concentrated upon relating Boserup's suggestion concerning the role of women in agricultural economies to the analysis of modes of transmitting property. Her stress on the role of women in shifting agriculture adds an important dimension to the study of the social implications of productive systems and enables us to suggest a model which reconciles her thesis with the devolution hypothesis.

While it is important not to overvalue the use of such techniques, the methods employed represent an advance that helps us to get a little beyond the circularity of structural functionalism and the much simpler unilineal, single-factor hypotheses that dog so much work in the social sciences. In this present case they help to map the various factors that are linked to diverging devolution

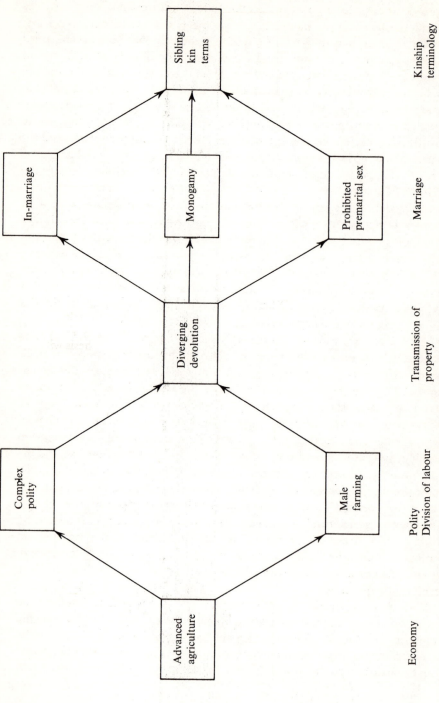

FIGURE 4. *Causal model: social implications of advanced agriculture*

Economy   Polity   Transmission of   Marriage   Kinship
     Division of labour   property   terminology

38

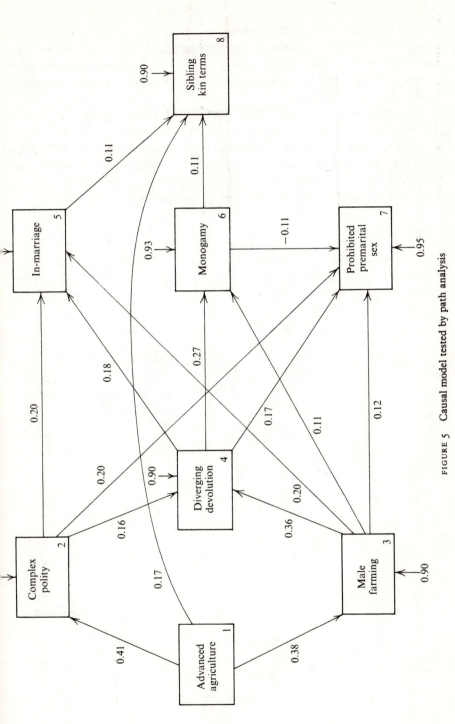

FIGURE 5 Causal model tested by path analysis

39

and are coded for a wide range of world societies. They are still far too crude, but at least such methods tend to reduce the arbitrary element in our assumptions and therefore to replace dispute by argument about theories which can be tested and improved rather than simply rejected in favour of a different set of assertions.

But these methods represent only one possible form of analysis, necessarily limited to factors that others have rendered more systematic. In the following chapters I turn to the more impressionistic procedures with which the social sciences are familiar to look at the kind of roles and role behaviour that one might expect to be associated with this type of devolution, this mode of organising the reproduction of domestic groups and of social hierarchies.

Note

A version of this chapter will appear in *Numerical Techniques*, edited by Clyde Mitchell, in the monograph series of the Association of Social Anthropologists.

5. Concubines and co-wives: the structure of roles in Africa and Eurasia

The phrase 'social structure' has carried a variety of different meanings, but the one with which I want to start is that used by Nadel in his *Theory of Social Structure*. Nadel attempted to outline a mode of analysing and comparing the inventory (or 'set') of roles in human societies, giving special attention to differences in the command over actions and command over resources (1957, 115). His analysis has not to my knowledge been pursued, nor do I intend to do so here, though not for lack of faith. My intention is more concrete, for it is to look at certain aspects of the structure of roles not only as a 'set' (i.e. from the internal standpoint) but in order to examine their articulation with other aspects of the social system (the external standpoint) as well as their implications for individual behaviour (the internalised standpoint). I do not wish to go into the merits of different approaches, structural or functional, to the study of society, since I do not think of these as alternatives. But I would suggest that we must try to get beyond the more simple-minded complexity of most writing in this area and try to link our efforts to the mainstream of social and historical thought, a not unimportant consideration for those who hope for cumulative advances in the social sciences.

Nadel derives the structure of a society 'through abstracting from the concrete population and its behaviour the pattern or network (or "system") of relationships obtaining "between actors in their capacity of playing roles relative to one another"' (1957, 12). The last phrase is a quotation from Talcott Parsons, but the idea is also expressed by Radcliffe-Brown.[1]

In this chapter I want to outline briefly some of the differences in the role compendia (or social structures, in Nadel's usage) of African and Eurasian societies (at least of the societies in Eurasia characterised by a relatively advanced agriculture). I accept Nadel's point that such role-systems have a certain measure of coherence (though 'fit' must be regarded as a variable) and I argue that this coherence relates in a significant degree to differences in the economy and the technology (including the technology of the intellect), though I would certainly not claim that they are completely determined by these factors.

The task of examining the distribution of roles in Africa and Eurasia is

41

altogether too vast, and it is not something to be attempted in a limited compass. But I want to try and offer some pointers to characteristic differences in role categories (that is, in the actor's classification of roles, the role labels) as well as in the associated behaviour, both approved and disapproved, and to elicit some reasons for these differences. The roles I shall deal with lie in the domestic domain, though they tend to get omitted from discussions of 'kinship' and 'kinship terminologies', which are often based on a curiously restricted notion of the total field, the artificiality of whose boundaries would be less important had not so much emphasis been placed on the existence of delimited sets critical in componential and other types of formal analysis.

Let me begin with the roles of co-wife and concubine. The major Eurasian societies show a definite trend towards monogamy, or at least to limited polygyny. This does not of course mean they are more moral, or more restrained, or more ascetic than African societies, where polygyny was practised in virtually all groups. For there have been many societies in Eurasia which institutionalised polycoity, either in the form of the concubine of earlier Chinese society or the handmaid of Ancient Israel. Indeed, there are others, notably in the Islamic areas, that permit plural marriages. But in this latter case, there is still a remarkable difference with Africa. In the latter continent, polygyny rates average 35 per cent of all marriages.[2] But the proportion of polygynous marriages is reported to be below 4 per cent in Egypt, 2 per cent in Algeria, 3 per cent in Pakistan and Indonesia.[3]

The great variation in these figures indicates that polygyny plays a very different part in the two areas. In Eurasia, it is largely, but not exclusively, an heir-producing device.[4] In this way it resembles other solutions to the problem of the absence of a lineal heir. For example, barren (or insufficiently fertile) women may continue to be accepted as wives while the absence of an heir is solved by bringing outsiders into a filial role (e.g. by adoption). Or barren wives may be divorced in favour of a more fertile one (giving rise to serial monogamy). Or such women may be supplemented by taking additional concubines (in polycoity) or wives (in polygyny). The first three solutions are largely Eurasian; the fourth, polygyny, largely African.

As the Biblical story of Sarah and Hagar illustrates, the failure of a wife to produce offspring after a reasonable lapse of time could be considered an incentive for taking an additional partner. But in Eurasia it was usually a handmaid, that is, a concubine, rather than a co-wife, whereas in Africa the status of spouse was usually indivisible. Although African wives may be differentiated by order of marriage, e.g. into first and second, senior and junior, right and left, great and small wives, they are all wives in the full sense of the term differentiated as wives.

The point can be made most briefly by referring to the terminology, though such evidence cannot represent the last word on this matter. Among many African peoples, there exists a word for 'co-wife', the root of which is often related to 'jealousy'. On the other hand there is no equivalent of the term 'concubine' that is so frequently used in discussions of domestic life in many of the major societies in Europe and Asia. At least, anthropologists have made no attempt to employ such a term to translate any specific word in the local language. This situation is the one that I found to exist among the LoDagaa and Gonja of Northern Ghana.

This has not been the case everywhere in Africa. Some writers have employed the term 'concubine' for various types of sexual union. Writing of the Nuer, Evans-Pritchard describes two forms of concubinage – widow concubinage and the concubinage of unmarried women. Widow concubinage can be seen as a more inclusive form of the levirate; that is to say, a woman for whom bridewealth has been paid continues to produce children in the name of her dead husband whether or not she is living with a close kinsman of the deceased. Such arrangements are also found among the LoDagaa of West Africa and the Zulu of South Africa, at least since the middle of the nineteenth century. After all, it is 'cattle that beget children' (Gluckman, 1950, 184). So that unless the new husband pays cattle, then the children belong to the lineage which originally did so. The basic principle behind the levirate and widow concubinage remains the same.

With regard to the concubinage of unmarried women the position is somewhat different. Since no bridewealth has been paid, the children belong to the mother's natal lineage, a situation which is again found among both the Zulu and the LoDagaa.

The critical aspect of both types of union described by Evans-Pritchard has to do with the determination of the social filiation of children on behalf of whose mother no bridewealth has been paid by the genitor. As I have noted, both situations are to be found among the LoDagaa and the Zulu (as among many other societies in Africa), but in neither of these cases have these unions been referred to as 'concubinage'.

I would argue that whatever terms we choose to employ, there are some fundamental differences between arrangements of this kind and concubinage as described for Asia and for Europe. In these latter cases the critical feature is the status of the woman rather than her children. Although the standard definition of concubinage refers to 'the state of a man and woman cohabiting as married persons without the full sanction of legal marriage', the position of the offspring may not be affected at all.

In this respect the general situation in Europe differed from that in Asia. In Europe, it was often difficult to distinguish a concubine from a spouse taken under that loose form of marriage, derived from Roman law, which was devoid of any public form and rested upon *affectio maritalis*, i.e. the fixed intention of taking a particular woman as a permanent spouse. This kind of marriage was preferred by early Christians to the more formal kind known as *confarratio* or *coemptio* because it was free of pagan idolatry. It was widespread in Scotland under the name of handfasting, but in England the pledge at the church door served a similar purpose.

In France unions were often of the informal kind, at least initially and at least among the peasantry. In the seventeenth and eighteenth centuries, while the daughters of the aristocracy and the bourgeoisie were theoretically kept in convents until the time of their marriage (thus at once preserving their honour and the authority of their parents at one and the same time), the daughters of the peasantry were either working in the house or going outside as servants. In some parts of France the evening gatherings at particular farms (*les veillées*) could end up with young men being permitted to stay the night with the daughters of the house; this tradition of 'coucher en tout bien tout honneur', the nocturnal visitation (*alberger*) was a kind of *fréquentation*. These *fréquentations* were intended to be chaste but like unions born in other circumstances, at fairs or in the woods, this was not always the case and premarital conception was sometimes the result. But pressure of village, church and law was behind forcing the seducer to marry the girl he had dishonoured. 'Les unions charnelles sous promesse de mariage . . . étaient considérées comme des "mariages de fait"', though they lost this character from the middle of the sixteenth century onwards, partly because of the stricter attitude of the church and partly because of the refusal of the royal courts to recognise this as marriage (Flandrin, 1975, 229–30).

But prenuptial arrangements might take more permanent forms than mere visiting. In Corsica, religious and civil marriage was only celebrated some months after the *abracia* or *embrassement*. This prenuptial concubinage, suggests Flandrin (1975, 184–6), may have been a very common preliminary to ecclesiastical benediction, the partners wanting to see if their marriage would be fertile.[5] However, such a state of affairs could continue if bride and groom fell within the range of prohibited degrees (i.e. if the union was 'incestuous'), although cohabitation was authorised by the church as a cause (albeit 'infamous' as distinct from 'honest') for allowing a dispensation if it were a subject of 'scandal' (Flandrin, 1975, 34, 100). And as far as 'custom' was concerned, such arrangements had the same kind of force as in medieval England and in Scotland of a later period. To speak of prenuptial conception in these cases is to adopt the position of the church and state, not of the actors. The increase in illegitimacy and in abandoned children seems associated with the cities, where the normative pressures were easy to escape, and with a period when both church and state succeeded in discrediting the local forms of hand-

fasting, bundling, concubinage, common-law unions and such like, and imposing their own ideology of marriage.

This kind of concubinage refers not to the taking of secondary sexual
partners of lesser status but to the type of 'formless' marriage that was first
approved by the church, then condemned by both church and state alike, a
type of marriage that in many places preceded the 'churching' of the couple,
equivalent to the binding betrothal that was so widespread in Europe and was
so recognized in its legal systems. In England, for example, the marriage of
Richard of Anesty was set aside by papal rescript in 1143, although it had been
celebrated in church and had resulted in the birth of a child, in favour of an
earlier marriage constituted by a mere exchange of consenting words (Pollock
and Maitland, 1898, ii, 370). However, such forms of marriage generally persisted in the rural and lower classes rather than in urban and upper groups.
It was the latter who were given dispensation for 'honest' causes, the former
for 'infamous' ones; the daughters of the bourgeoisie and the aristocracy were
more carefully protected than those of the peasants.

Considering how to distinguish such informal marriages from concubinage,
the medieval canon lawyer, William Lyndwode, fell back on a definition of an
earlier canonist. If the woman eats out of the same dish as the man, and if he
takes her to church, she may be presumed to be his wife; if he sends her to
draw water and dresses her in vile clothing, she is probably a concubine.

In addition to 'formless marriage', Roman law recognised concubinage
(from the verb 'to lie with') as a legal status; it was admitted as such by the
early Christian church, providing a man had no wife; and in the thirteenth
century, the great English lawyer, Bracton, treats the 'concubina legitima' as
entitled to certain rights.[6]

Concubinage was also recognised by many early civil codes in Europe. In
Germany 'left-handed' or 'morganatic' marriages were allowed by the Salic
law between nobles and women of lower rank. In different states of Spain the
laws of the later middle ages recognised concubinage under the name of
barragania, the contract being lifelong, the woman obtaining by it a right to
maintenance during life, and sometimes also part of the inheritance with the
sons ranking as nobles if their father was a noble. In Iceland, the concubine
was recognised in addition to the lawful wife, though it was forbidden that
they should dwell in the same house.

Another confusion between concubinage and marriage was caused by the
gradual enforcement of clerical celibacy. During the bitter conflict between
laws that forbad sacerdotal marriage and customs that allowed it, legislators
often spoke of priests' wives as concubines and attempted to reduce them to
an inferior position; clerical concubinage replaced clerical marriage. The position of priests with regard to marriage has a general significance for the study

of the status of spouses, since it throws some light upon the differences between Africa and Eurasia. Why were priests dissuaded from marriage? There is, of course, a strong element of self-denial in Christianity, particularly in the Pauline version. Similar ascetic traditions are found throughout the Eurasian continent, and reach their apogee in the monastic institutions of medieval Europe and of Tibetan Buddhism. But we have also to remember that the maintenance of the church as an organisation, the church as a corporation with its specialised priesthood, the church of literate societies rather than the less substantial church of Durkheimian sociology, such an organisation requires its own property. To maintain a complex hierarchy of priests requires a large endowment. Such property may be brought into existence through labour or it may be acquired by force. But the major means by which church property in Europe became as substantial as it did was probably by gift and by inheritance. Both meant an alienation from family heirs, the denial of kinship that Christ demanded from his followers. If priests could not marry, there could be no competition for their property; concubines and their children inherited only to a limited extent. Moreover, 'celibacy' could profitably be extended to the laity. Individuals of means might be persuaded to leave property to the church; widows and heiresses who entered a nunnery became, like other novitiates, the brides of Christ, and the conjugal fund (their property) was aggregated to the church. It was above all the church that promoted the right of women to inherit land, for it was through them in particular that the church benefitted.

In Europe then there was much confusion in the use of the term concubinage for (i) unions of the customary kind (by 'mere word of mouth', as Pollock and Maitland put it), which the church was nevertheless forced to recognise. In this category too were later placed sacerdotal marriages in the course of the long struggle to reduce their status. The use of the word concubinage was part of a process of imposing new forms of marriage by the church and later the state. (ii) unions of a secondary kind entered into by the partners knowing this to be less complete than other forms of marriage. Such unions may be first marriages that limit the rights of spouse or of children (as in 'morganatic' marriages). More usually however, and these are the forms in which I am particularly interested, concubinage is secondary in another sense because it takes the form of making an additional union with a partner of different, indeed lower, status.

The difference of status is clear from the words of the Koran, which observe that the wife has her father as protector, while the concubine is defenceless against her husband; in China concubines usually came from a distance so that kin ties were ineffective. The difference in status is often related to differences in the nature of the marriage transactions and whether or not the spouse had been endowed with her own property. One of the reasons why the Turkish Sultans began to take concubines rather than wives was the cheapness of such arrangements, as compared to the huge state weddings together with the indirect dowry or dower, with which he had to endow his bride.

The difference in status is implicit in the marriage contract and it is significant that these differences took a written form in what is virtually the earliest known legal code, the code of Hammu-rabi, which emanated from the area in which what I have called complex polities and advanced agriculture first appear to have developed. In this code, a full marriage, bestowing the *assatum*, involves a written contract. 'A woman who has been taken to wife does not acquire the rights and liabilities of an *assat awilim* ... unless a *riksatum* has been given to her by her husband' (Driver and Miles, 1952, 247). The acquisition of the role of *assatum* is mentioned in the first sentence in several of the small number of marriage contracts that have been preserved, and it is followed by the penalties to be paid by either spouse for repudiating the other.

This early example draws attention to the fact that concubinage exists in precisely those Eurasian societies, the areas of the 'great civilisations' descended from the Mesopotamian, Egyptian, Indian and Chinese societies of the Bronze Age, that we looked at earlier. Concubinage is found predominantly in those Eurasian societies where some kind of dowry prevails, societies which are also mainly monogamous or where plural marriages represent a small proportion of the total. Marriage in the full sense refers to those cases where the wife is endowed with property; concubinage on the other hand is propertyless.[7] Indeed the concubine may be a form of property. For in ancient Israel, as in more recent times in the same area, the term concubine was often used for a slave wife. Here there is an important difference with Europe, since the status of the children is not at stake. A free man could acquire a slave girl for the purpose of sexual gratification, just as he could purchase a male or female slave to do all kinds of work inside the home. Such a slave girl retained her servile status but her master was not supposed to sell her, and especially not if she had borne him children. The children of a concubine had the same status as the children of full wives. They inherited in the same proportion, and if a man had no child by a wife, the child of his concubine inherited his status, position, and occupation as well.

In other words concubine here means slave wife; in ancient Israel the status of a slave who has slept with her master changes automatically. Deuteronomy (21.10–14) gives precise regulations for the case of a man who seeks to take a female captive. After coming to his house she must shave her head, pare her nails, put away her clothes and bewail her father and mother for a full month, after which her master may take her as a spouse. Having done this, if a man wishes to put her away, he cannot sell her 'because thou hast humbled her'. In Arabia, the same custom obtained. 'In the time of the prophet', wrote Robertson Smith, 'when a woman became pregnant by her captor it was no longer proper that she should be sold in the market or ransomed by her people for money' (1907, 90).

Note that a woman could also acquire a 'servant' (*'ebed*') and indeed might bring one with her in marriage as part of her dowry. If the wife is barren the 'handmaid' might be employed as a substitute. When Sarah saw that she bore no children to Abraham, she asked him 'to go in unto my maid', Hagar, the Egyptian, in the hope that she, Sarah, 'may obtain children by her' (Gen. 16.1–4). The position was obviously full of conflict. When Hagar bore a child, she began to despise her mistress who drove her out (though she returned to bear Ishmael, who in turn begat twelve princes, and of whom God said 'I will make him a great nation'). While the concubine was of low status, her child was fully legitimate and could be the founder of a lineage. Patai suggests that when the handmaid became pregnant it was believed her powers of fertility could pass on to her mistress and she, too, would become pregnant (1959, 41–2). To ensure this, the handmaid gave birth to her child upon the knees of her mistress (Gen. 30.3). But we need to interpret this custom sociologically rather than magically. The handmaid is clearly substituting for the wife, as also in the case of Rachel who gave Bilhah to Jacob, and of Leah when she stopped childbearing, hence the legitimacy of the children she bears is unquestioned.

In China, too, we find a sharp distinction between wives and concubines; bigamy, which can be an offence only in a monogamous system, was a crime as early as the T'ang dynasty. Van der Valk notes one interesting exception; where a man has inherited leadership in two distinct though related unilineal kin groups, each of which maintains a separate shrine and rites, he could marry twice, once in each kinship personality, giving a separate heir to each of the groups he headed (1956, 44). Otherwise a man could only add to his holding of women by taking a concubine, that is, by contracting a lesser form of conjugal union. In China such unions were comparatively rare; in an extensive survey in the 1930s, one in eighty wives were found to be concubines.[8] Clearly there were a variety of reasons behind the act of taking a second sexual partner. But the most prevalent recalls the role of the handmaiden of the Old Testament in providing an heir for a barren couple. This being the case, it is essential that even though the wives are differentiated in status, the children of the secondary spouse are fully legitimate. Otherwise they could not act as heirs.

In Japan, monogamy pervaded and concubinage of the Chinese type was abolished with the promulgation of the Criminal Code in 1880. In India, monogamy was recognised as the ordinary and natural mode of marriage (Westermarck, 1921, iii, 45), but the *smritis* allowed a man to have concubines (*dasi, bhujisya*), in addition to full wives; these women were married without 'due form' and could not be heirs to their husbands.

Here the problem of concubines was complicated by the existence of endogamous castes. Basing his analysis on early Hindu law, Mayne has little to say on the subject of concubinage, although he distinguishes eight different forms of marriage, beginning with the Brahma (the gift to a man learned in the Vedas) and continuing to Pisacha, 'when the lover secretly embraces the damsel, either sleeping or flushed with strong liquor, or disordered in her intellect' (Mayne, 1892, 81). However, observation of actual practice shows that the institution exists. From the North Indian village of Rampur, Lewis reports a form of marriage known as *jhar phuna* which is used by 'lovers and people who are too poor for a regular marriage ceremony. The man and woman leave the village and build a fire of dry grass and twigs. Then they return and live together as man and wife' (1958, 190). A yet more interesting form is described by Dumont for the Pramalai Kallar of South India under the specific heading of concubinage, although as with Lewis the author himself encountered no examples of such a marriage in the course of his fieldwork, testifying to its rarity. Of this *vaippatti* union Dumont writes that it was known not only to the jurists of old but to people generally. Only after a man had made a full marriage could he enter into such an arrangement, the difference consisting in the absence of all marriage ceremonial. He was told that such a marriage could take place under two circumstances. Firstly when the woman belonged to another caste; in this case regular marriage would have brought excommunication, but not concubinage. Secondly when the wife was of the same Kallar caste but a man did not want to upset the children of his first marriage, who would be concerned to retain the property which belonged to the original conjugal fund. 'Allez-vous-en, nous ne vous donnerons rien' . . . ('ils considèrent donc que leur père n'a pas le droit de soustraire au profit d'une nouvelle union des biens qui doivent leur revenir') (1957, 182). Hence a rich man could provide a separate house for his concubine, even endowing her illegitimate children with some property, though her status is always a despised one.

Note that in the Pramalai Kallar case, concubines are not only rare but their children are illegitimate. This difference with China may be connected with the different emphases placed upon adoption. In India adoption was widespread, which may have avoided in some measure the resort to a secondary sexual partner to provide an heir. Whereas in China, the institution of adoption was looked upon somewhat ambivalently. In the township in the southwest of the country studied by Hsu (1949), adoption was not regarded as the most favoured method of securing continuity; and in approximately one-third of the cases of clan rules studied by Mrs Liu (1959) a negative attitude was reported towards the adoption of outsiders.

However this may be, both forms of 'inferior' union are clearly connected with the trend towards monogamy. Among the Pramalai Kallar the pressure towards concubinage arises from the fact that the husband committed his property to the conjugal fund established at his first marriage and the members of that group ('le premier lit') whose interests are threatened. Only a rich man can make further full marriages.

It is interesting to observe that the reasons for not undertaking a second full marriage are very similar to those which in parts of Europe militated against the remarriage of a widow. For example it is recorded of Hyères, Var, that a *charivari*, a form of ritualised hostility known in England as 'rough music', was sometimes organised by the adult son of a widow when she was getting remarried. 'Le but était de protéger "les intérêts des enfants du premier lit"' (Remiremont, Vosges); 'les enfants d'un premier lit ayant souvent à pâtir du second mariage, d'où le péjoratif: marâtre' (Cahors, Lot) (Thompson, 1972, 311).

Let us now return to the position of the so-called concubines in Africa. There it was the filiation of the children that was primarily at stake. A similar situation arises in the case of the alternative marriage arrangements of the Ijaw and the Nyamwezi, where the attachment of children to the father's or mother's group depends upon whether or not bridewealth has been paid at the parent's marriage. No doubt bridewealth and non-bridewealth marriages are differently evaluated, but this does not appear to be reflected either informally or formally in the status of the spouse. In any case, the status differs from the concubine in Eurasian societies, a woman who is taken in some lesser form of marriage without property or even as a slave. Indeed concubinage in this latter sense seems linked to dowry systems where women are differentiated in terms of the property attached to them, a situation which again is strongly associated with monogamy, or at least with limited polygyny.

I do not want to deal at any length with the possible reasons behind the distribution of single and plural marriage, partly because of space and partly because I have touched upon them elsewhere.[9] But it is impossible altogether to avoid the problem.

A number of authors (e.g. Heath, Boserup and Clignet) have related polygyny to the economic role of women in hoe farming; by marrying another wife, a man gains another labourer in his fields. We have seen earlier that the distribution of polygyny and monogamy is associated with simple and advanced agriculture but have related this to other factors. The kind of status differentiation that accompanies an increase in production and a scarcity of land is seen as encouraging the settlement of property on women as well as on men. One form the settlement takes is the endowment of women at marriage, which tends to dominate the kind of union they make. The dowry they receive is 'matched' with property brought by the husband, the conjugal contributions creating one fund as well as one flesh, though clearly other valued qualities may be relevant in any particular transaction. From the prospect of this type of marriage, the major escape is elopement (Martinez-Alier, 1972, 1974).

Monogamy (with or without concubinage) seems to be widely associated with these systems of 'diverging devolution' because it is difficult to repeat this type of funded marriage, since the spouses have to commit their property in order to get a partner of the right standing. Under these conditions, a second (polygynous) union is most likely to occur when the original couple are without heirs, that is, in a situation where a monogamous society might resort to divorce and remarriage. The women in such secondary unions are less likely to be endowed with property and hence more likely to be concubines. In Africa, on the other hand, there are no such constraining factors to inhibit the tendency for men to accumulate women in sexual partnership.

In other words, to start by trying to explain polygyny is to start from the wrong end. As far as human cultures are concerned, it is monogamy that is rare, polygyny common, anyhow until recently, though of course it was the larger, more advanced societies that displayed monogamous tendencies. However in this context it is the consequences, not the cause of polygyny and monogamy in which I am interested, especially the implications for role structure and role behaviour. They are associated with the differences in the status of spouse, with equal co-wives as against unequal concubines. Both situations give rise to jealousy. Leah (the hated one) quarrelled with her sororal co-wife Rachel (the beloved): 'Is it a small matter that thou hast taken my husband?' (Gen. 30.15). Equally, Sarah became jealous of her handmaid, Hagar. Nevertheless the status difference is significant on both psychological and social levels. The establishment of a conjugal fund (in all its various forms) in which both wife and children have rights, indeed to which the wife has contributed from her portion, means that each subsequent marriage has radical effects upon the position of the existing wife and children. Concubinage separates sex from property and allows for the addition of 'inferior' spouses for intercourse or for procreation.

In polygynous societies of the African kind there is no inhibition on adding full wives. In this context married men often act towards women as potential husbands; they adopt courting behaviour which is consistent with a form of 'diluted marriage' (to adapt a phrase of Stephens). Moreover, the institution of widespread polygyny is sustained by a large differential marriage age, later for men than women (though permanent bachelorhood would do as well), which may create problems for the young males. In any case the domestic organisation is going to be more complex and domestic relationships more diffuse when many households consist of a plurality of wife/mothers, at least for a part of their cycle of development. In this context I want to draw a contrast between the classificatory role of 'mother' as found in Africa and the individualised mother of Europe, where relationships established by second marriages are distinguished by special verbal forms. In India, though step-parenthood is clearly significant, partly because of the allocation of property to each marriage (Mayne, 1892, 522; Dumont, 1957, 182), no terminological distinction is made; however, as elsewhere, the qualification 'elder' and 'younger' distinguish classificatory from linear parents.

'Mothers' and step-mothers

Just as we find the concept of concubine absent among the LoDagaa, the Ashanti and the Tallensi of West Africa, at least as a named status differentiated from that of wife, so too there is no distinct word for step-parent. In Europe step-parenthood comes about through the death or divorce of a spouse, and refers to the relationship established by a new spouse with the children of his or her predecessor. Terminologically, there is no duplication of the mother role, which is allocated to one individual and one only. Clearly, the usage implies monogamy. But it goes further and implies that successive spouses cannot replace one another. From one standpoint this is more generally true. The role of mother and father, whether socially or biologically defined, is usually regarded as irreplaceable. Hence the Tallensi, while using a category term for 'father' which includes 'father's clansmen of the same generation', nevertheless recognise the uniqueness of the parental bond in a number of ways. The importance of the status of 'not having a father' is extensively discussed by Fortes; it refers not to the loss of 'fathers' in general, but to the loss of the individual who is acting as *pater* and who is essentially incapable of being replaced. So too among the LoDagaa a number of critical rituals performed on children when their parents die have to do with their newfound status of 'orphan' (*bikpibe*).

But despite the undoubted individualisation of a specific father role within the general role category of 'fathers', a point I earlier discussed in analysing the mother's brother (1959), the very existence of this wider role-category is in itself significant. For it means that a man has other 'mothers', other 'fathers', who can take over part at least of the role – and with the minimum of dislocation. For in Africa, where polygyny is common, parental terms are used in a classificatory sense. That is to say, a man's wives are called 'mother' by his children. Equally, when a woman remarries, either after divorce or after widowhood, her children refer to her new husband as 'father'. In monogamous systems, this usage is impossible; the mother's husband, or the husband's new wife, are classified in a different way than the father or mother hemselves. The reason is partly connected with the uniqueness of the property arrangements made at a particular marriage. In a polygynous society with patrilineal inheritance, the children by any of the father's wives will tend to be equal with regard to the property of the male progenitor. But in dowry societies, where the property has been allocated to both the woman and the man at their marriage, the beneficiaries of this property will be the children of that particular union. Any new marriage will necessitate a degree of protection of the children of either of the spouses by a previous marriage. Hence the concept of step-parenthood and step-children, which differentiate the members of the two nuclear families created by 'serial monogamy' in a very different manner than the feature of 'complementary filiation' in a polygynous patrilineal society differentiates the children of two wives (Fortes, 1949b, 1959).

The role of a step-parent is clearly critical in dowry systems. In *Sense and Sensibility* Jane Austen presents a typical step-situation. Henry Dashwood inherits his uncle's property and passes it entail to his son by his first marriage. His second marriage has produced three daughters who are living with him in the family home at the time of his death. Shortly afterwards, the son, John, arrives at the house to take up residence. He had been enjoined by his father to treat his step-mother generously, but his wife persuades him to cut down his financial contribution to a paltry amount. During this discussion, both he and his wife constantly refer to the father's second wife as 'mother-in-law', which as the *Oxford English Dictionary* informs us was then in frequent use for step-mother. The French too have a single term for step-mother and mother-in-law, namely, *belle mère*, reflecting perhaps a network of canonical prohibitions. But they also have another, special word, *marâtre* (Spanish, *madrastra*, also meaning 'something disagreeable'), to describe the cruel (or 'wicked') step-mother, a term not of address or reference but rather of fairy-tale, where the suppressed or implicit aspect of the relationship can be projected in story.

Once again the point can best be brought out by referring to the equivalent situation in Africa. If a woman who has already had children marries for a second time, there is no conflict over property (though there may be other reasons for tension) between the male offspring of the different fathers. The daughters of the different unions all have some interest in their mother's estate, but it is usually small. If the mother dies, the children by the first husband will return to their paternal home, if they have not done so already; the others may suffer as 'orphans' but hardly as step-children; in any case, a polygynous family has no one step-mother and any hostility will be diffused.

In dowry systems one of the consequences of direct inheritance is that the woman's property will be divided between the children of her various mar-

riages and the new husband may well prefer that only his offspring should
inherit her property, to the exclusion of the children of his predecessor. Like-
wise a step-mother might wish to benefit her own children at the expense of
her husband's offspring by an earlier marriage. Such considerations presumably lay behind the fears that were so often expressed in Europe about step-
relationships, from Juvenal onwards.

> Wives loathe a concubine's offspring. Let no man cavil
> Or call such hatred abnormal: to murder your step-son
> Is an old-established tradition, perfectly right and proper.
> But wards with rich portions should have a well-developed
> Sense of self-preservation. Trust none of the dishes at dinner:
> Those pies are steaming-black with the poison Mummy put there.
> Whatever she offers you, make sure another person
> Tries it out first: let your shrinking tutor sample
> Each cup you're poured.
>
> (VI: 626–34).[10]

Here we have epitomised the role of the wicked step-mother, when looked at
from the standpoint of the dead mother or her children; it is the domestic
counterpart of what Gouldner has called the Rebecca situation. And in terms
of witchcraft accusations, one would expect the step-mother in Europe to
replace the co-wife in Africa.[11]

It is of significance here that the prime example of the step-situation, that is,
the Cinderella story, is largely a European tale; Cox gives 134 versions of type
A, of which 114 contained ill-treated heroines; only 3 of these tales are of
Asian origin.[12] The central element of the plot turns on the ill-treatment of the
heroine, which is later reversed by a hypergamous marriage. As Lang puts it,
'a person in a mean or obscure position, by means of supernatural assistance,
makes a good marriage' (1893, vii); this position is reversed in *Puss in Boots*,
where it is the ill-favoured hero who marries up. In this respect the two
themes complement one another. In 78 of the European Cinderella stories, it
is a step-mother or step-sister who ill-treated a young girl; in the remaining
33 cases, the step-mother was replaced by:

sister(s) in 18 cases,	cousins in 1 case,
mother and sisters in 6 cases	father in 1 case,
mother in 4 cases,	foster mother in 1 case,
parents in 1 case,	indeterminate in 1 case.

The instrument of the reversal of Cinderella's fate, the opponent of the
step-mother, is the god-mother, that is the fairy god-mother (that useful
encapsulation of Christianity and paganism). In one interesting version from
the Italo-French border, it is the fairy god-mother who marries the heroine's
widowed father, thereby becoming her step-mother as well; in the process her

personality changes from beneficent to cruel. Miss Cox's summary of the story reads: 'Heroine persuades her widowed father to marry her fairy god-mother, who has prompted her to do this, saying it will make her happy. Heroine is kindly treated till step-mother has two children; after that she is sent to mind the goat and is set task, to spin a pound and a half of hemp.' It is this goat who in the end helps her to marry the prince (1893, 124–5).[13]

Writing of these stories, Andrew Lang concludes, 'One thing is plain, a naked and shoeless race could not have invented Cinderella. Beyond this I cannot go' (1893, x). From the advantage of a wider perspective we may venture beyond this overtimid conclusion, for it is also plain Cinderella could not have been invented in a society without step-mothers or hypergamous marriage. Marriage up the hierarchy had to exist, at least as a dream of the servants' hall, even if an infrequent occurrence; indeed the mobility that emerges from the narrative might have served to mitigate the effects upon individuals of a comparatively immobile society, like Hindu beliefs in the changing of roles in the afterlife and beyond.

It is not only women who fall into this category of evil stereotypes. Why is it that we have wicked uncles as well as wicked step-mothers? A system that channels male property to women encourages direct inheritance, the distribution of property to children rather than to collaterals. Direct inheritance inevitably raises the problem of the minority and the protection of the childhood heir. The problem is greater when we are only dealing with succession to an indivisible office rather than with potentially divisible property.[14] But the obvious regent (or caretaker) for the heir is the father's younger brother; his position of trust then puts him in a position to switch the inheritance to his own line.[15]

As far as succession is concerned the story of the English king, Richard III, provides the classic case.[16] For inheritance, a popular example is found in that well-known ballad, *Babes in the Wood*. The story turns on the death of 'a gentleman of good account' from Norfolk and his wife, leaving behind two infants, a boy and a girl. To the modern reader, who has learnt the story in childhood as a 'fairy tale', their fate is probably more familiar than their situation, since childhood concentrates on its own. However the critical factor was the status of these infants as wards of a close kinsman who was also the residual heir.

> The father left his little son
> As plainly did appear,
> When he to perfect age should come,
> Three hundred pounds a year;
> And to his little daughter Jane
> Five hundred pounds in gold,
> To be paid down on marriage-day,

> Which might not be controlled,
> But if the children chanced to die
> Ere they to age should come,
> Their uncle should possess their wealth;
> For so the will did run.

Their uncle, the wicked uncle, was the father's brother, who having hired two ruffians to seize the children and abandon them in a wood, was visited by the anger of God, which laid waste all his lands and caused two of his own sons to die. Eventually the evil man died in jail, where he had been sent for debt. The final verse offers a fitting moral, warning off those wicked men who would try to sequester the property of others.

> You that executors be made,
> And overseers eke,
> Of children that be fatherless,
> And infants mild and meek,
> Take you example by this thing,
> And yield to each his right,
> Lest God with suchlike misery
> Your wicked minds requite.[17]

The wicked uncle, as the father's brother, tends to be contrasted with the maternal uncle, who is good, and often a safer guardian for a ward (Homans, 1941, 192; 1951, 252ff.). While there may be general psychological factors behind the allocation of virtue to the mother's side, we are here concerned with more mundane considerations. In Africa, where so called bifurcate merging terminologies predominate, the father's brother is classified as a father. There is no question of complete identity and, as we have seen, the existence of kinship categories is not inconsistent with a recognition of the importance for an individual of 'not having a father'. Nevertheless, the father's brother tends to be treated as the father, and while hostility may develop between the generations, wickedness is not perceived as a characteristic of the relationship. If the father's brother inherits the property, and even the widow, this is a normal part of lateral transmission (widespread in Africa), not the sequestration of property destined for someone else's children.

Spinsters and bachelors

Having touched upon the problem of step-parenthood and the related question of guardianship, I want to return to co-wives and concubines by dealing with two other roles which display a somewhat similar distribution, namely those of the bachelor and the spinster. It is clear that a high degree of polygyny such as exists in Africa could be maintained by a high percentage of bachelors, i.e. never-married males. Given such abstinence on the part of the many, the few can enjoy plenty. But in Africa, the situation is not like this. Nearly every woman and every man get married, despite the high degree of polygyny.[18] I do not claim that there is no concept of the spinster or bachelor in Africa; the LoDagaa for example have the words *daa kuor* and *pɔɔkuor*, though the latter can refer to any woman who has no husband, even a woman about to be married leviratically. But there is no institutionalised role for the unmarried. Western Europe was quite different in this respect, and has been ever since the sixteenth century and possibly before. In that region, as Hajnal (1965) has pointed out, the general pattern is a late age of marriage for both men and women as distinct from the pattern that maintains extensive polygyny by means of the late marriage for men alone, i.e. a high differential marriage age together with a large proportion of never-marrieds. In Table 23 are the figures Hajnal gives for Belgium and Sweden for the year 1900.

TABLE 23   *Percentage single at selected ages*

	Men			Women		
	20–4	25–9	45–9	20–4	25–9	45–9
Belgium	85	50	16	71	41	17
Sweden	92	61	13	80	52	19

Contrast the figures from Eastern Europe, which come closer to the African situation:

	Men			Women		
Bulgaria	58	23	3	24	3	1

These are dry figures; the human implications of the position of the elderly spinster is most graphically and cruelly conveyed in Roy Fuller's line 'The filthy aunt forgotten in the attic', which he recently mentioned in the *Times Literary Supplement* when commenting upon the ancient problem, of anthropology as much as literature, of the contrast between meaning assigned by actor and by observer. 'A picture, of course', claimed one critic. 'No', replied Fuller, 'a person.' The actual explanation seems more likely to lie in a recollection of that traditional Scottish song, 'An Auld Maid in the Garret', the words of which I reproduce because of their insight into this typically 'European' situation.

> Noo I've aft times heard it said by my faither an' my mither,
> That tae gang tae a waddin' is the makins o' anither.
> If this be true, then I'll gang wi'oor a biddin'.
> O kind Providence won't you send me tae a waddin'
> For it's Oh, dear me! whit will I dae,
>   If I dee an auld maid in a garret.

Noo there's ma sister, Jean, she's no handsome or goodlookin',
Scarcely sixteen an' a fellow she was coortin'
Noo she's twenty-four wi' a son an' a dochter
An' I'm forty-twa an' I've never had an offer.

I can cook an' I can sew, I can keep the hoose right tidy
Rise up in the morning and get the breakfast ready
But there's naething in this wide world would mak' me half sae cheery
As a wee fat man that would ca' me his ain dearie.

Oh, come tinker, come tailor, come soldier or come sailor,
Come ony man at a' that would tak me frae my faither.
Come rich man, come poor man, come wise man or come witty
Come ony man at a' that would mairry me for pity.

Oh, I'll awa hame fur there's naebody heedin'
Naebody heedin' tae puir Annie's pleadin'
I'll awa hame tae my ain wee bit garret –
If I canna get a man than I'll shairly get a parrot.

In France too, the number of spinsters was very high in the big towns, especially in the rich quarters where there were many servants. A similar surplus appears even in the smaller towns, whereas the villages were left with an 'excess' of bachelors (Flandrin, 1975, 66, quoting Bourdieu, 1962).

This situation with regard to never-marrieds is clearly consistent with certain other social institutions. The first of these is the existence of sacred spinsters and bachelors, those who have consecrated their life to religious ends, denied themselves personal continuity and sexual pleasure in order to further the religious community and to follow the ascetic path to grace. Neither monasticism nor a celibate priesthood are features of Africa, south of the Sahara. Indeed in the absence of an advanced agriculture it is doubtful if complex organisations of this kind could be maintained.

Secondly, it is consistent with that system of preferential primogeniture which in some European areas allowed younger brothers or sisters to stay on the family land as long as they did not marry (see Homans, 1941; Arensberg and Kimball, 1940; J. Goody, 1976). In such societies the role of the unmarried daughter was often to look after her father and mother when they became old and incapacitated.

Thirdly, it is consistent with the obligation to stay unmarried which was a feature of various forms of rural employment, either for males on the land (Habbakuk, 1955a) or for females in domestic service (Flandrin, 1975). As Hajnal has pointed out, the situation was not substantially changed by the industrial revolution; for one of the main sources of labour in the growing industrial towns of Europe was the pool of unmarried women who came to work in order to accumulate a dowry. The female surplus due to immigration was larger in the big commercial centres (e.g. Nuremberg, Frankfurt and

Basle) than in smaller towns (Hajnal, 1965, 124). Contemporary Africa presents a contrast; there it is the women who are often left behind while the men go to town,[19] sometimes to accumulate bridewealth, though they often go after marriage. The difference may be related partly to the nature of the available jobs and type of industry; it may also be related to the greater contribution made by African women to agricultural production (which is part of a general contrast between plough and hoe agriculture).[20] But one factor is surely the absence of a type of marriage that requires the accumulation and matching of property. Indeed this matching of property may mean that marriage involves the settlement of the farm on the groom, and lands or cash on the bride, that is, the effective transfer of the basic productive resources at marriage rather than at death. How does this affect the age of marriage and hence the possible existence of a phase of spinsterdom or bachelorhood in an individual's life-cycle? Hajnal rejects Homans' suggestion that such marriages, which produce the type of stem household characteristic of many parts of Europe,[21] necessarily meant a late age of marriage for men. He notes that over half the children in thirteenth-century England may have lost their father before they reached their seventeenth birthday. If they all married on their seventeenth birthday and the remainder immediately after their father's death, there is no reason to think that the average age of all men at first marriage would have been above 24. In fact, of course, as Homans documents in detail, many were married during their father's lifetime when the father turned the land over to them (1941, 144). Nevertheless, 24 is already 'late'; and in such a system, the age of marriage of the heir or heirs is likely to rise as the death rate is lowered. The handing over of one's kingdom, as Lear found out, can be done too early;[22] so there is likely to be some pressure towards the late marriage of men, and sometimes of women.

A late age of marriage tends to encourage the existence of life-long spinsters or bachelors, who often fill specific roles. One such is the role of maiden aunt, more likely to exist where there is the usual differential age of marriage in favour of men, combined with a low sex ratio and low divorce rates. The very idea is associated with female renunciation; unmarried men seem more likely to move outside the household into monastic or other institutions than in the case of unmarried women, who are more likely to move into other people's households as servants, as 'maids'. In this role, they provide a reserve of domestic service, which may or may not be separated from the giving of sexual services (the difference between the concubine and the 'maid'). Or they may remain as a spinster in their natal families. Finally, where these admit women, they may go into monastic institutions.

The acceptance of celibacy and of a late age of marriage is clearly linked with other important features of the outward and inner life of those who

belong to these societies. For the postponement of marriage does not obliterate
the sexual desires of men or women, though it may suppress or sublimate
those drives. Despite the pressures of society, and their internalisation by
individuals, men nevertheless sought out women for the pleasures of sex, and
the result was often pre-marital pregnancy. Where the man and woman concerned were 'equal', a marriage might well follow; the phenomenon of bridal
pregnancy was frequent in parts of England and in parts of France (Hair,
1966; Flandrin, 1975). But where the status of the two was unequal (as sometimes between master and servant, a situation where domination could easily
be transformed into sexual access), marriage might well be impossible, so that
pregnancy would be followed by abortion, infanticide or the abandonment of
the child. As far as women were concerned, the main culprits, as revealed in
legal proceedings, were not married masters, but bachelors who were unable
to provide for a girl, either because they were priests (in sixteenth century
France, 'filles à prêtres' was as common an expression as 'filles à soldats' became
later), already married or else unmarriageable bachelors, 'domestiques agri-
coles incapables de constituer le pécule nécessaire pour faire vivre une famille,
et peut-être peu désireux d'accéder à l'angoissante situation de manouvrier'
(Flandrin, 1975, 208, 214); it was these bachelor domestics who 'constituted
a permanent risk for village chastity, of girls, widows or married women,
especially in the farms where they were working' (245). These were the wolves
in the rural 'bergerie', the seducers of girls themselves away from home, in
service, though the latter were even more at risk in towns where the pressure
on a man to marry the girl he had dishonoured was substantially less.

Monogamy, celibacy and late marriage affected not only behaviour between
the sexes but, by repressing the usual expression of sexual desires, encouraged
the resort to masturbation, homosexuality, bestiality and dreams of a sadistic
character. While for girls, 'le désir des hommes, même s'il les fascinait, leur
faisait peur, et leurs propres pulsions refoulées engendraient logiquement des
phantasmes masochistes. Ou bien elles rêvaient d'un autre monde où le coït
n'engrossait ni ne déshonorait: le monde diabolique du sabbat' (Flandrin, 1975,
170).

Of course renunciation took 'positive', sublimated forms as well as 'negative',
repressive ones; thus late marriage not only drove women to the towns or to
service to accumulate a dowry, it also encouraged members of both sexes to
practise a work ethic that compensated in some measure for early 'chastity'
(Flandrin, 1969, 1972).

Once again, as with step-parenthood, the difference in the distribution of
spinster and bachelor roles is one between Africa and Europe, indeed Western
Europe. In Asia, women all tend to get married, though for some men the
denial of sexuality is a road to grace. The rejection is particularly marked in

Buddhist societies; in Tibet the number of spinsters is augmented by the practise of polyandry. And among certain upper caste Hindus, women might formerly be discouraged from marrying – partly because of the dowry that would be involved in finding them a husband of the right standing. The same tendencies that we find in Western Europe appear in Asia in a more subdued form.

Conclusions

I have been dealing here with certain roles that are absent from one type of society (the hoe agriculture of Africa) and present in the other (the advanced agriculture of Europe and Asia). Absent, that is to say, as specific named positions, or what I have called role categories. But it is also the case that even roles that are found in both types of society differ in significant ways for the same reasons. For example, the mother–child bond is inevitably influenced by the presence of plural marriage and classificatory motherhood; for one thing, it is more diffuse. The reasons that lie behind this situation influence other ties, such as that between brother and sister, brother and brother, as well as between a man and his parent's siblings e.g., his mother's brother. I cannot here go into these differences, except to refer to a discussion in the context of conjugal and affinal relationships that appears in a recent contribution to a book on *Bridewealth and Dowry* (Goody and Tambiah, 1973). In societies which place an emphasis on monogamy and on dowry the situation with regard to affinity or in-lawship will differ significantly from those in which there is bridewealth and high polygyny. For example, in those societies (or classes) in which such conjugal arrangements prevail, a premium is placed not only on monogamy but also on low divorce, since just as it is difficult to duplicate such marriages, so it is difficult to dissolve them. Difficult but not impossible and high rates of divorce are found in some Arab countries; logically female inheritance would give greater freedom than pre-mortem transmission in the shape of dowry, which is tied to marriage. In such cases there may well be inhibitions on widow remarriage. A fund is often seen as established once and for all, and it is a fund in which husband, wife and children have a joint interest of some kind.

One early example from ancient Israel will bring out the nature of the conjugal fund and its bearing upon the role of women. During the 1961 excavations in the cave of Letters in Nahal Tever, a cache of documents was found belonging to a certain Babata, which included deeds for the sale of palm groves, deeds of gifts and debts, many other legal papers and two marriage deeds (*ketubot*). Babata had married twice, and had inherited properties from her parents and from her two husbands. One of the legal documents concerned the appointment of guardians for her son by her first husband. One of the marriage deeds concerns her second marriage to one Judah, where the 'bridal price' is 'a hundred Tyrians', the traditional sum for a widow or divorcée. The other deed relates to the marriage of her step-daughter. The dowry agreed upon by the two parties was two hundred silver denarii, and the bridegroom undertook to 'owe this sum to ... his wife, together with another 300 denarii'. What is happening here is that the dowry the wife brings is increased by a larger donation ('indirect dowry') from the groom, though both sums stay under the control of the husband until his death.

This property arrangement clearly indicates the continuing interest which both husband and wife have in the conjugal estate. Indeed in a deed for the sale of a house dating from the second century A.D., the wife specifically renounces any claim. 'And I, Salome, daughter of Shim'on, wife of this Heder, I have no claim against the sale of this house, forever.'[23]

Obviously affinity here is a more permanent, individualised relationship than it can be in a polygamous society, especially one where divorce is common. For with plural marriage, alliance (in the sense of generalised relationship between the 'groups' involved in marriage) is likely to be more hesitant, more fragile, more temporary; a man is unlikely to get much help from a wife's brother unless the union with the sister has a relatively high probability of persisting, and unless it is also an individual one. In this context, however, it is worth returning to the step-mother in order to draw attention to the fact that the categorisation of in-law relationships in Europe was in certain respects wider than in Africa, just because the mother/wife category was narrower. In Europe the father's second wife was often classified as an in-law, whereas in Africa she is a mother. From one standpoint, both categorisations are connected with the extension of marriage prohibitions to father's wives. The in-law system incorporates close affines as quasi-nuclear kin (mother, sister, brother, etc.) who thereby become unmarriageable. Hence step-mother and mother-in-law were often interchangeable categories.

Let us look back at differences in the structure of roles that we have tried to establish between Europe and Asia on the one hand, and Africa on the other. There is the stress on concubines as against co-wives, an emphasis on single as against plural marriage, with all that means in terms of commitment and 'love'. Clearly it affects the nature of conjugality, psychologically and economically, since the making of one flesh is also the creation of a single enterprise. But it also affects the structure of domestic groups. The taking of wives serially rather than contemporaneously splits the sibling groups not only by maternal origin but also by age and current status of wife. This is connected with the problem of the step-mother who replaces the co-wife as a figure around whom tension accumulates. In Europe successive spouses of a man or woman are differentiated with regard to their respective offspring; they are not mothers but step-mothers. In Asia, with its less insistent emphasis on monogamy, successive wives tend to be classified as 'mothers'; however women, at least in the upper castes, cannot take second husbands, so that the concept of step-father is excluded from consideration. In Africa, both mothers and fathers are part of a wide category that includes parent's siblings of same sex as well as parent's other spouses. Polygyny then is closely related to the way kin are conceptualised, to the actor's picture of the set of kinship roles.

Other roles we referred to briefly were those of the spinster and the maiden aunt, the step-mother and the wicked (paternal) uncle as against the good (maternal) uncle. But there are also many important differences in the existence or presence of other roles. Take, for example, the influence of marriage policy on the role of the elder and younger brother in rural France. In any peasant society, there is always the possibility of marriage to an heiress, that is a daughter who has no brothers and will therefore inherit the farm. For a younger son (a *cadet*), such a union enables him to stay in the region and to escape from poverty and celibacy. Interestingly enough, according to Bourdieu, the younger son in late-nineteenth-century Béarn was not likely to be excluded by his elder brother. The latter tended to marry younger sisters in families that were equal to or slightly above their own, because to marry an heiress would make them divide their energies on two separate farms. Meanwhile, heiresses looked for a younger son from a good house.

But such a marriage was not without its difficulties for the cadet, as many proverbs testify. The heiress was likely to lord it over her husband, thus reversing the 'normal' hierarchy.

> Qui se marie par intérêt, de sa femme est le valet (Catalon).
>
> Héritière, tête d'oisel (Béarn).

The marriage of the eldest son was more closely controlled than that of his younger brothers. At the same time he was normally favoured as the future head of the agricultural enterprise, even being treated differently at the table (Flandrin, 1975, 63). However, his marriage had to be made for the benefit of the household; it was the younger brothers who could marry 'for love' rather than for reason, who were less subject to the parental will, better able to experiment and choose for themselves (Flandrin, 1975, 64, 243).

Again the property situation affected the problem of widows and orphans. If marriage is delayed through the necessity of acquiring property (e.g. for the acquisition of a new home when there is a taboo against two married couples living in one house), then the problem of orphanhood is increased; and if men delay more than women (i.e. increase the differential marriage age), then the problem of widowhood becomes more widespread. If widows are allowed to remarry, then their acquisition of the conjugal property makes them attractive partners and one gets the phenomena of the 'merry widow', typified in Chaucer's 'Wyf of Bath'. This is the *feme sole*; she has been paid off by her brothers at her marriage (diverging devolution complicates the cross-sibling relationship; it is 'dishonourable' not to provide an adequate dowry for one's sister) and by her husband at his death (and hence requires no support). In the Middle East, the husband's brother could sometimes inherit in the levirate, but in contrast to the African situation, this happened only when a man had no offspring; like concubinage, it was essentially an heir-producing device.

Monogamy may also take the form of the prohibition, or at least the disapproval, of the remarriage of widows. In Africa, we do not know that widows are ever prevented from taking another spouse. Instead, the high rate of polygyny both causes and is caused by widow remarriage. That is to say, a high rate of polygyny depends upon a large differential marriage age (DMA) between men and women. Hence more widows. It also depends upon younger (or rather surviving) men taking these widows as spouses, by the levirate, by inheritance or by non-selective remarriage. In Eurasia there is a greater tendency in the other direction, partly because this is a statistical consequence of monogamy, but also because of social factors, the binding nature of the union in ideology and the binding nature of the union in property. The same factors militate against separation in lifetime and hence tend to produce low rates of divorce, as in India, in Europe and in the Far East. Once again the contrast with Africa is very clear; though divorce rates vary against a range of factors, such as system of descent groups, size and nature of bridewealth, etc., rates are universally high compared to the other two continents. 'Among the Brahmans', writes Dumont, 'marriage tends to be unique (monogamous) and indissoluble' (1966, 110).

Outside the kinship sphere we have the persons involved in arranging suitable matches, namely the go-between, in addition to the chaperone whose job is to prevent the unsuitable ones. More directly connected with the wider rather than the domestic economy, we have pointed out that in Africa there was slavery but no serfdom, rulers but no landlords, subjects but no tenants (J. Goody, 1971a). In the next two chapters we shall examine in greater detail the distribution of adoption and its relation to strategies of heirship in societies that restrict plural marriage.

What I have tried to do in this chapter is to bring out some of the differences in roles that are associated with the simpler agricultural systems of Africa on the one hand and the more complex agriculture found in much of Europe and Asia on the other. 'In the last resort' ('the lonely hour of the last instance', as Althusser puts it), these differences are based upon the economy, though factors to do with the polity, with stratification, with systems of communication are clearly of major significance. The link between stratification and the economy is by means of the system of inheritance, which organises the transmission of property from generation to generation, at death, at marriage or at some other point in the developmental cycle. It is these factors that lie behind (though they certainly do not completely determine) the differences in the structure of social roles that have emerged in the context of co-wives and concubines.

6. Adoption in cross-cultural perspective

Adoption plays a major part in the traditional law of many Eurasian societies. It occupies a large portion of Mayne's *Treatise on Hindu Law and Usage* (1878). The Babylonian code of Hammu-rabi, the oldest comprehensive set of written laws, gives a prominent position to 'Adoption and Wet-nursing' (Driver and Miles, 1952, 383–406). And the institution receives the same kind of attention in the law of China, Greece and Ancient Rome. Theoretically it has been of central importance in the writings of Sir Henry Maine and Fustel de Coulanges, where it is linked to the perpetuation of corporations of agnates over time.

In recent years much work has been done on the structure of such kinship corporations (usually known as unilineal descent groups) in Africa and elsewhere (e.g. Fortes, 1953) and, directly or indirectly, the work of Maine and Fustel de Coulanges has played some importance in the seminal studies of segmentary lineage systems in Africa.[1] It is remarkable therefore that adoption is rarely, if ever, mentioned in these accounts of African societies; the institution is not discussed at all in the important studies by Evans-Pritchard of the Nuer (1951) and Fortes of the Tallensi (1949b).[2] The situation of the Ashanti seems typical; legal analysts and sociological observers agree that adoption as such is not known in Ashanti law (Allott, 1966, 194).

What are the reasons behind this uneven distribution of adoption and how are they linked to other broad differences between the major Eurasian and African societies? First we have to specify the functions of adoption, for even where it is found, the institution can fulfil very different roles. Mayne remarks on the surprise felt by many 'commonsense Englishmen' on hearing that Hindu law forbade the adoption of orphans (1892, xii). This distribution again needs to be explained.

The institution of adoption, whether considered comparatively or not, must be looked at in the context of other quasi-kinship relationships such as fostering, godparenthood, etc.[3] A general examination on these lines has been undertaken by Esther Goody in the context of a study of fostering and her paper 'Forms of pro-parenthood: the sharing and substitution of parental roles' (1971) is an essential complement to this; it was as a result of her work that

66

I looked again at the problem of adoption in connection with this more general comparison of Eurasian and African societies. The comparative survey will necessarily be less than comprehensive. I know of no attempt to discuss the distribution of adoption; it is not included in the data in the *Ethnographic Atlas* (1967) nor in Goode's study of changing family patterns (1963). I shall try to summarise the forms of adoption in the major historical civilisations of Eurasia and contrast these, in a general way, with the situation in Africa, south of the Sahara.

While one concern of this comparative study is theoretical, the other is practical. A noteworthy aspect of development in West Africa has been the tendency to treat social problems in the same way as the economy is treated, i.e. by the importation of European models and know-how. Mental hospitals are established to deal with psychiatric troubles: remand homes are introduced to deal with recalcitrant youths; state pension schemes are worked out to deal with the aged, and adoption laws are formulated to safeguard the interests of the parties concerned. In universities, social administration courses are started by expatriate staff on expatriate lines, using handbooks written for social workers in Brooklyn or Birmingham.

In a recent report on 'Women's Work' in Ghana (*Advance*, 48, October 1965, 4) the following are listed as the main topics that the social education programme should consider;

1. The importance of the family unit.
2. The social weakness of separated homes and its repercussions on the children.
3. The need for the development of the sense of parental responsibility in the interest of the children.
4. The importance of a satisfactory family life in the interest of sound mental health.
5. The need for co-operation and co-ordinated effort in the interest of the growing child.
6. The problems of the school-going child.

The whole orientation is towards the 'ideal type' elementary family of Western Europe, with little apparent attention to the nature of existing institutions or to the costs of the implied changes.

Much of the concern with Western institutions is no doubt necessary; the movement to new urban centres does pose greater (and certainly different) problems from those that were present earlier. But there are three main objections to the Euro-centred approach of politicians, civil servants and social administrators. First, know-how about social problems is essentially different from technological knowledge; the former is largely guess-work, the latter experimental; and whereas it is unlikely that a new nation will come up with a better way of making motor-cars, it could easily improve upon the treatment of delinquents. Second, such a possibility is yet more likely when the European 'solution' does not take full cognisance of local conditions. The failure to understand the underlying situation may mean the expenditure of considerable sums of money on 'solutions' that are less adequate than they need to be; and the corollary is that substantive problems may be neglected, with huge social and economic costs. For example, it is quite conceivable that the economic growth of a developing country could be completely swallowed up by the cost of social services if the major responsibility for maintaining the aged is switched too quickly from a specific family commitment to a general state provision: yet whatever Eurasian model is adopted, the new nations are impelled by slogans such as 'pensions for all' into taking the latter course.[4]

Hence it seems important to examine what is meant by European terms such as 'adoption', to identify the institutions and their functions, to understand their distribution and, if possible, their correlates, for the purposes of social action as well as social theory.

The functions of adoption

In Western Europe, adoption has three main functions:

(i) to provide homes for orphans, bastards, foundlings and the children of impaired families;
(ii) to provide childless couples with social progeny;
(iii) to provide an individual or couple with an heir to their property.

These functions often overlap; since the last two (the last is a special case of the second) centre upon the adopter, and the first upon the adopted, they are not necessarily incompatible. The title of a recent book on fostering in Britain, *In Place of Parents*, indicates that the welfare aspect of the institutions of adoption and fostering is the one most stressed in contemporary Western cultures; that is, the first of the functions mentioned above – the care of deprived children. In pre-industrial societies, however, it would be more appropriate to entitle a book on this topic, 'In place of children', since it is parental 'deprivation' that has the edge. Of Roman adoption Crook writes, 'it had nothing to do with the welfare of children, and those adopted were often adults' (1967, 111). A consideration of parental needs is not absent from European society: the childless couple is the one most likely to fulfil the welfare function. It is rather in the third aspect, the provision of an heir, that the major difference lies.

Adoption defined

This point is most clearly made by a comparison with Roman society where the English term originated, the root implying choice, option. But before doing this it is well to consider what is involved in the act of adoption. It is not generally realised what a relatively new phenomenon legal adoption is in England, where the Adoption Law dates from 1926 (James, 1957, 39ff.). Nor is the scale of the problem with which the welfare services have to cope in finding parental substitutes recognised. In Great Britain the average illegitimacy rate is 5–7 per cent of the birth rates (9.3 per cent in 1945) and it is estimated that at any one time 150,000 children in the country are in need of 'care and protection' (Kornitzer, 1952).

Adoption is defined by the *Oxford English Dictionary* as taking someone into a relationship not previously occupied, especially as one's own child. In English law the effect of an adoption order is that the child 'should rank for legal purposes as the child of its adopter and cease to be regarded as the child of its parents' (Johnson, 1965, 293). This was also the situation in Roman law. An adopted son was cut off from his natal family and became (for most legal purposes) the son of the adopters.

The act of adoption, both in Rome and in Britain, involves the transfer of an individual from one filial relationship to another, from a 'natural' relationship to a 'fictional' one, but one which is in most respects legally equivalent. In other ways, it clearly is not the same. In Rome, for example, an adopted son still had to observe the prohibited degrees of marriage attached to his earlier status.[5] In fact an individual is only in a position to break off all ties with his natal kin when he is adopted as an infant and when the parents conceal his 'natural' filiation; this is likely to happen only in the European instances of type (ii) (of adoption by childless parents) where the adopted child is an emotional substitute for the parents and is transferred in infancy; even then discovery of the 'natural' relationship is almost as inevitable as the accompanying crisis.[6]

If complete transfer is virtually impossible, legal or jural substitution is feasible in a majority of social contexts. Noting that many authors have not been too clear in the usage (often confusing 'adoption' with 'fosterage'), we reserve the former term for those cases that approximate to the Roman and British in terms of rights relinquished and acquired.

Rome

In the Roman case, however, the context in which adoption is found contrasts with contemporary Europe. Crook describes adoption during the Republican period in the following terms:

the characteristic remedy for a family in danger of dying out was adoption, and that was the primary purpose of the institution ... Anyone with a spare son was in a strong position to link his family with some other noble house by giving him in adoption ... There were ... really two institutions of very different origin; adrogation of a person *sui iuris*, which always required public sanction, since such a person was in principle head of a family (whether he actually had one or not) which, along with its cult, would suffer extinction by being merged in yours; and adoption in a technical sense, the transfer of someone *alieni iuris* from the *potestas* of his or her *paterfamilias* into yours.[7] A man adrogated brought all his property and descendants across with him automatically; a man or woman adopted came by themselves, leaving their children (if any) under their original *paterfamilias* – and of course they would have no property to bring (1967, 111).

The separation was radical. In the case of adoption, a man became a stranger to his natal agnatic family and in the case of adrogation he renounced the worship of the gods of that family by the act of *sacrorum detestatio*. He took over new gods and it was said of him, *in sacra transit*, he has passed into the worship of the new family (Fustel de Coulanges, 1955, 55; Buckland, 1932, 124; Schulz, 1951, 145). The separation was also irreversible in that an adopted son could not of his own will rejoin his natal kin, even when they were in difficulties. The two great families of the second Punic war were forced to continue their lines by adoption. The grandson of Fabius Maximus and the son of Scipio Africanus adopted brothers, the sons of L. Aemilius Paulus by his first wife Papiria, whom he had divorced. The situation turned out tragically for Aemilius Paulus, because the two sons of his second marriage both died in their youth. Given the state of hygiene and medicine, the extinction of the line was always a factor to be reckoned with; yet large families are liable to be a drag on the inheritance.

The completeness and irreversibility of the act, its possible consequences for giver as well as receiver, indicated that it was never lightly undertaken. The conditions under which transfer could take place were significant. As far as adrogation was concerned, Cicero argues that only a man who had no children could undertake this. 'What, gentlemen', he asked, 'is the law relating to adoption? Clearly, that the adoption of children should be permitted to those who are no longer capable of begetting children, and who, when they were in their prime, put their capacity for parenthood to the test.' And he attacks the adoption (*adrogatio*) of Clodius, which also had political implications, as contrary to sacerdotal law because the adopter already had a son: 'the father, by the act of adoption, will disinherit his son.'[8] Ulpian also seemed to think that it was undesirable for people to take such an action if they had legitimate children alive or were still capable of having them. As Buckland notes, '*adrogatio* destroyed a family and thus was only allowed to save another, i.e. to provide a *heres*' (1932, 125).[9] The rules are less limiting with regard to *adoptio*, but such transfers are again hedged about with safeguards and conditions.

Adrogation, said Cicero, disinherited a son. In a more general sense adoption, like written testaments, set aside the 'intestate' heirs, a man's agnatic kinsmen. It provided an individual with a son and heir, one who could inherit his property, continue his line and perpetuate his worship. As Cicero again remarked, the inheritance of property and the worship of the dead were intimately associated in Roman society; for this reason a man wanted to provide himself with a specific descendant to carry out both these tasks.

Consequently it was those with most to inherit who were most concerned to provide themselves with an heir. There were other reasons for adoption in Roman society; an uncle might adopt an orphaned nephew. But mainly the institution was one whereby the great families provided themselves with heirs to their property and worship, successors to office or a political following (*clientela*). From Julius Caesar and Augustus onwards, a considerable number of emperors, failing to beget sons, adopted them instead (Balsdon, 1962, 210). For this purpose, males had to adopt males, even close agnates; women could not adopt, though they could be adopted (not adrogated). But in both cases it was not the deprived but true citizens who were adopted, often the sons of other big families. For the giver there was a gain in the shape of an alliance between the two houses, while the recipient perpetuated his own line.

Greece

Similar institutions existed in ancient Greece. Adoption in classical Athens occurred when a man had no offspring at all or when, having no sons, he wanted to prevent a close kinsman from claiming his daughter as an heiress (*epikleros*).[10] If he had a daughter he would find her a husband and then adopt either him or one of his sons; men adopted their grandsons or (as in China) their agnatic nephews, and sometimes their nieces to succeed as *epikleroi*.

Adoption could be carried out either *inter vivos* or posthumously by will.[11] During a man's lifetime, his adopted son was presented to the phratres and the demesmen; after death, the claim had to be established by court action.

Adoption was thus mainly of close kin, though sometimes of affines.[12] No one would adopt who had a legitimate son of his own and if he begat a son after the adoption had been arranged, the 'natural' and 'fictive' sons would share the property between them.

The adopted were cut right off from their own kin and entered fully into the status of son, except that they were unable to make a will and could therefore perpetuate their new *oikos* only by direct descendants. However, there was one condition under which an adopted son could return to his natal kin, that is, when he in turn had begotten a son. But if he did this, he cut himself off from his own progeny.[13]

Such an instance is illustrated by Demosthenes in the speech 'Against Leo-chares'. Archiades had died without issue, leaving a brother, Meidylides, and the grandson of a sister, called Leocrates. Under Athenian law, the brother was to be preferred as the intestate heir, but he was out of the country at the time. Leocrates had himself recorded as the adopted son of the dead man and entered into possession of the property. The brother returned, angry at what had been done, but was persuaded by his friends to acquiesce. Mean-while Leocrates transferred the estate to his own son Leostratus, who was in turn incorporated in Archiades' clan and deme, leaving his father free to return to his own family. Leostratus did the same with his son, Leocrates II, who died without issue. A case was then brought by the brother's lineal descendants claiming the property.[14]

The status of an adoptee also differed in that he could be more easily repudiated than a 'natural' son. Moreover, as in marriage, a citizen could only adopt a citizen, for only citizens could own the *oikoi* of Athens; it was in any case only males who could adopt, though girls were sometimes adopted as heiresses (Isaeus XI, 8). Adoption involved a continuation of the worship of the family shrines and this too could not be properly carried out by a foreigner. An adopted son had to look after his adopter in his old age, bury him when he died and worship him after his death. Even more perhaps than in Rome, the practice was connected with continuity, both of property and worship, in the direct line of descent.

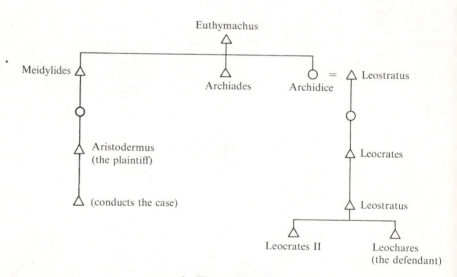

FIGURE 6   The adoption of Leocrates.

Hindu India

The Indian situation was much in the minds of nineteenth-century writers engaged in reconstructing the early history of their institutions, mainly because of certain assumptions concerning the social and ethnic unity of the Indo-European speech community. But it is a vast continent with a long and literate history, whose practices are not easily summarised in a few pages. The difficulties in describing the place of adoption in Hindu usage are well illustrated in Mayne's compendium (5th ed., 1892); the presence of law-books written over many centuries and the existence of great variations in local custom make any general statement liable to a considerable degree of error. Nevertheless, of the importance of adoption there can be no doubt at all, whole books of law being devoted to the one topic; Mayne himself allocates a total of one hundred and seventeen pages to the subject, a significant proportion of his whole book.

Ancient Hindu law discusses twelve sorts of sons, 'all of whom are competent to prevent a failure of obsequies, in the absence of filiation; the highest in status appears to have been the son of the 'appointed daughter' (*putrika putra*), one who had entered into a *sarvasvadhanam* marriage, with the words, "I give unto thee this virgin, who has no brother, decked with jewels; the son who may be born of her shall be my son"' (Mayne, 1892, 80). Such a marriage could take place when a man had no male heirs, but some texts suggest that the child of any heiress might be automatically placed in such a position and that men were warned against marrying a brotherless girl lest her father should take her first son as his own.

The 'appointment' of a daughter had the effect of providing an individual with an heir who could continue his line and inherit his property. The same effect was achieved by adoption (*dattaka*) and this is virtually the only one of the twelve alternative forms of sonship to survive (Mayne, 1892, 79). 'The perpetuation of the lineage', writes Mayne, referring to a man's personal line of descent, 'is the chief object of adoption under the Hindu law' (161); and the probability is that any sonless Hindu will turn to adoption (170).[15] By this act, the adopted son entered into a new inheritance and its concomitant obligations, but he still retained a minimal link with his natal family, since he was debarred from marrying there (179).[16]

The conditions placed upon adoption again make its functions clear. According to Manu, the adopter must have no son and the boy must belong to the same class. Vasishtha adds that an only son cannot be adopted, that the act must have the consent of the kinsmen concerned and indeed that the adopted son must be 'a boy nearly allied to him, or (on failure of such) even one remotely allied ... The class ought to be known, for through one

son the adopter rescues many ancestors'.[17] And this end may be achieved
even after a man's death for a son can be adopted to his name, though
this ghost-adoption can be initiated only by his widow.[18] 'The reason',
remarks Mayne, 'probably is, that she is looked upon not merely as his
agent, but as the surviving half of himself, and, therefore exercising an
independent discretion, which can neither be supplied, nor controlled, by
any one else' (1892, 123). However, this can only be done when husband
and wife have established an independent conjugal estate: 'a widow, who
has not the estate vested in her, and whose husband was not separated at
the time of his death, is not competent to adopt a son to her husband
without his authority, or the consent of his undivided coparceners' (137).

The adopted son should be as close as possible to the adopter, preferably a
brother's son who, as in China and Greece, is the preferred kinsman.[19] The
adoption is carried out by means of a specific ceremony, which, among
Brahmans, includes a burnt offering (data homam). The essential element is
the giving and receiving; after the religious service, the adopter asks the
natural father: 'Give me thy son', and the other answers: 'I give him.' He
receives him with these words: 'I take thee to continue the line of my ancestors' (Mayne, 1892, 162). Despite the emphasis in this text upon the religious
aspect of the ceremony, among lower castes this particular element is not
necessary to establish adoption, contrary to the opinion of those earlier writers,
like Sir Henry Maine and Fustel de Coulanges, who saw religion as the matrix
of law and emphasised the relationship of adoption to the ancestral cult. J. D.
Mayne argues persuasively that 'Notwithstanding the spiritual benefits which
are supposed to follow from the practice, it is doubtful whether it would
ever be heard of, if an adopted son was not also an heir. Paupers have souls
to be saved, but they are not in the habit of adopting' (1892, 102). They
have, of course, nothing to offer.

TABLE 24   'Sons' recognised in early Hindu law (Mayne, 1892, 68)

The legitimate son (aurasa)
The son of an appointed daughter (putrika putra)
The son begotten on the wife (kshetraja)
The son born secretly (gudhaja)
The damsel's son (kanina)
The son taken with the bride (sahodha) (i.e. a pregnant bride)
The son of a twice married woman (paunarbhava)
The son by a Sudra woman (nishada) or by a concubine (parasava)
The adopted son (dattaka)
The son made (kritrima)
The son bought (kritaka)
The son cast-off (apaviddha)
The son self-given (svayamdattaka)

In the frequent and intimate association between property and the ancestral cult, I follow Mayne in seeing no reason to treat the religion as the
independent variable, even in the context of adoption.

In treating of adoption in India, we can supplement ancient law with present
practice, and for this purpose I turn first to an account of the contemporary
legal position. In his *Introduction to Modern Hindu Law* (1963), Derrett writes:

A child may be adopted (rarely – subject to special conditions – an adult), and in this way an
orphan or a child of a relatively poor family may be given a good home and security. In practice
however Hindus have tended to adopt in order to fulfil needs prevailing in the family of
adoption. The need for a male heir capable of managing the estate and protecting the adopting
father's surviving spouse or the adoptive mother herself has resulted in adoption being confined
to sons. It has also resulted in a lack of power to adopt more than one son concurrently, and in
the right of adopted sons to upset alienations of joint-family property and to demand a share
in the corpus . . . (1963, 94).

But we need to supplement rules of urban courts and codes with the norms
of rural life. According to Madan's account of the Pandits in rural Kashmir
(1965), less than 4 per cent of children were adopted, usually when a couple
decided they were not going to have any children of their own, for these particular Brahmans do not approve of the Sanskritic injunction that a man may
marry a second wife in the lifetime of his first wife, if the latter fails to bear
him a son (82). Here adoption is a functional alternative to polygyny. A childless widow may also adopt a son to her dead husband's name, in a 'ghost-
adoption' that parallels the 'ghost-marriage' of the Nuer. Occasionally
daughters may be adopted, but the Pandits say 'adopting a daughter is like
rearing a pariah dog in the hope of obtaining wool'.

The most eligible male for the purpose of adoption is a brother's son or
failing that a more distant agnate,[20] but daughter's sons, sister's sons, and
wife's brothers were also selected. At the ceremony of adoption the natural
father places the boy in the lap of the adoptive father as a mark of the
transfer of kinship status, a ceremony that resembles the Biblical transfer of a
child from a slave girl to her mistress (Gen. 30.3). The adopted son becomes
the full legal child of his new 'father', but with the same exceptions that
obtained in Rome; he could not marry any woman prohibited to him in his
earlier status, nor did he lose an estate that had already been vested in him as an
individual (86). Again, adoption and inheritance in the direct line are closely
interlinked.

China

The importance of adoption in China is noted in many discussions of the legal
system. The position is clearly laid out by Mrs van der Sprenkel: 'Another
method of ensuring the continuance of the family was by the adoption of an

heir. That this was done deliberately with a view to providing for the succession to the line of descent is indicated by the term used to describe this type of adoption, *ssu chi*, to continue the succession . . . If a man had no son by either wife or concubine he was required by law to adopt an heir, selected according to fairly clear rules from among agnates . . . Only if there was no suitable lineage-member available for adoption as an heir (and a member of the same generation was not considered suitable) could an heir be taken from outside the lineage, and this would be recorded in the lineage genealogy, so that rules of lineage exogamy would not be infringed' (1962, 16).

Other forms of adoption exist. Foundlings may be given the name of the family that is looking after them; but they do not inherit. For women, there is the 'foster daughter-in-law' form of marriage, whereby a young girl is 'adopted' (or rather fostered) as a prospective bride.[21]

In addition males from other clans were sometimes adopted; merchant venturers might adopt sons to send out on trading expeditions (Freedman, 1966, 7). But in the main, adoption, in the full sense of the word, meant the acquisition of a son by an heirless male from among his close agnates.

In her study of the clan rules recorded in 151 genealogies, Mrs Liu notes that there is an obligation on the childless man to adopt and the adoptee had normally to be a clansman of junior generation. Moreover 'the ideal is to adopt an heir very close to the original descent line' (1959, 72). Indeed, 'closely related kin with an eye on the property of the adopting family would often force their son upon it' (73). On the other hand, the rules of 51 clans display a negative attitude towards the adoption of outsiders (75). For adoption is closely tied to inheritance and 'disputes of adoption are in reality disputes of inheritance' (76).

In some areas, such as the township in southwest China studied by Hsu, adoption was not the most favoured way of securing heirs, though it was still practised. A man is most likely to adopt the son of a brother or paternal cousin. The brother's children are already residual or 'intestate' heirs, who would share the estate of a sonless person; but if a man adopts one of them, he keeps the property intact and provides himself with the prized personal continuity that is part of the ancestral worship (1949, 76).

But elsewhere adoption is more favoured and exists side by side with the heiress (or 'appointed daughter') alternative. Of the village of Taitou, Yang writes that 'adoption is closely related to inheritance. As long as the deceased has a son, the problem of adoption does not arise, but if a man has no sons the adoption of an heir is imperative. The male line must be continued. The adopted heir is always the next of kin, or the father's brother's son' (1947, 83). Alternatively a son-in-law may take the place of a son by marrying his wife at her parents' house, i.e. by making an uxorilocal union to an epiclerate.

In southeast China in-marrying sons-in-law and adopted sons are again functional alternatives. Of the latter Freedman writes: '... if a man lacked a son, he was in the eyes of the law obliged to adopt one from among his nearest agnates in the generation next below his in order to provide a legally satisfactory substitute in the interests of succession to the cult' (Freedman, 1966, 7).

Adoption of males is in the main a way of creating an heir who will also act in a filial capacity after the death of the holder. As in the other cases we have discussed, a man can (and here frequently does) adopt a 'son' who is already a close agnate, a member of the same clan and lineage; there is thus no increment to the descent group as such, only a perpetuation of a man's own particular continuity through the purchase of an heir with the promise of property. While these are not the only considerations behind adoption in traditional Eurasian societies they bulk large in any discussion; with them in mind, I return to reconsider Maine's treatment of this subject.

Maine on adoption

It is since the publication of Sir Henry Maine's *Ancient Law* in 1861 that the institution of adoption has played a prominent part in the comparative sociology of kinship, his interests in the subject having in fact preceeded his experience as a jurist in India. Maine saw adoption as an example of a legal fiction, defined as 'any assumption which conceals, or affects to conceal, the fact that a rule of law has undergone alteration, its letter remaining unchanged, its operation being modified' (1931, 21–2). And he sees the fiction of adoption as one of the means whereby society took 'its first steps towards civilization', because it permitted the incorporation of strangers as kin and thus progressed from an emphasis on the bonds of kinship to the ties of contiguity as a basis for common political action. In Rome, he notes, 'the primary group, the Family, was being constantly adulterated by the practice of adoption, while stories seem to have been always current respecting the exotic extraction of one of the original Tribes...' (1931, 107). This practice was so important, according to Maine, because it 'permitted family relations to be created artificially' and by this means incoming groups could be grafted to native stock.

The phenomenon Maine describes, namely, the attachment of immigrant lineages to a locally dominant descent group, has been analysed in a number of detailed ethnographic accounts of African societies. Among the Nuer of the Southern Sudan, stranger groups are linked by a variety of ties to the core lineage of a particular tribe (Evans-Pritchard, 1940). Attached lineages among the Tallensi of Northern Ghana are frequently joined to others by matrilateral ties, the founding ancestor of the sub-dominant group being represented as a sister's son of the founder (Fortes, 1945, 50); in other

cases the passage of years seems to have brought about a more complete merging of the two groups, so that they now form one stock, at least in some contexts
of social action.

I hesitate to describe this process as adoption, since it is a retrospective
attachment whose rationale is an existing kin relationship. Nor do I know of
any sociologists who have compounded this 'political' procedure for the attachment of groups with the more precise acts that involve the deliberate transfer
of an individual from one group to another in order to fill a new kinship status
(though of course this transfer may, as in Rome, have political implications
of a different kind).

Adoption in this latter sense has somewhat greater affinities with the incorporation of slaves in societies like the Ashanti of West Africa; one of the
effects of the prohibition on enquiry into a man's origins is the same gradual
disappearance of servile origins that, in other societies, is carried out by formal
progression through a series of graduated stages.[22] But it differs in certain
major respects. As with the attachment of stranger lineages, the process is a
long-term one; it is 'concealed' rather than 'deliberate'; and it is concerned
with the creation of a new social personality rather than the transfer of a man
from one kinship status to another.

Maine discusses adoption, 'the factitious creation of a blood-relationship'
(1931, 161), in this more usual sense when he examines testamentary succession. 'Both a Will and an Adoption threaten a distortion of the ordinary course
of Family descent, but they are obviously contrivances for preventing
the descent being wholly interrupted, when there is no succession of kindred
to carry it on.' But this discussion seems to miss the vital point that in the
societies Maine considered, the kindred, gens or wider 'family' (i.e. lineage)
never automatically provided the heir (though the agnates were often the
'intestate' or residual heirs); if a man had no children and had property, then it
was customary to employ a legal fiction like adoption to appoint one. But a man
adopted to continue a descent line, not a descent group.

Maine's emphasis on the so-called adoption of strangers clearly derives from
his idea of the major long-term change in man's political development as the
evolution of society from one based on kinship to one based on contiguity.
Adoption is seen as a mechanism in the process of transition, a legal fiction that
permitted the revolution to take place imperceptibly. But in fact there is no evidence to show that a radical shift of this kind ever occurred, for all known
societies employ the 'principles' of both kinship and contiguity in the recruitment and organisation of social groups – though industrial societies certainly
place less emphasis than others upon extensive ties between kin. Hence it was
unnecessary to introduce adoption as a legal fiction (in the strict sense), since
there is no evidence that the 'principle' of contiguity was ever wholly absent

from human society.[23] In this context one should note that when sociologists describe adoption as a legal fiction and when Maine himself later characterises adoption as 'factitious', the terms are not used in the same way as in evolutionary contexts, since they refer to a means of enforcing rather than of changing the law; for adoption, 'social fiction' would perhaps be a better phrase, locating the process unambiguously in the actor frame of reference.

Maine's treatment of adoption, with the emphasis on social change rather than inheritance and worship, was connected with his container model of unilineal descent groups, the box-like corporations of agnates ('the family'), firmly bounded and minimally differentiated, whose extent is not specified and whose functions are all-embracing. In the course of promoting the 'Patriarchal Theory' he erected an 'ideal typical' group which he (and others) claimed had existed under the ancient law of India, Greece and Rome. It consisted of a band of agnates, under an all-powerful head, holding property in common and passing it down by universal succession. This group acquired its wives by purchase, disposing of its daughters in the same way. In a corporation of this sort, inheritance should clearly be automatic, not simply residual, and should pass down the line of brothers in turn. But, contrary to the model, brothers did not inherit from one another and the devolution of property was basically lineal, going to sons by inheritance and daughters by dowry.[24] The idea of large corporations within whose boundaries all major operations were carried out bore little resemblance to the Rome known from documentary sources. But convinced that this later Rome represented a development from an earlier and purer type of agnatic corporation, Maine (and later Fustel de Coulanges) painted a picture to suit the theory. Included in this picture was the idea of adoption as an instrument of change away from pure agnation.

In China, India, Greece and Rome, adoption had little to do with the incorporation of strangers or with augmenting the strength of the unilineal descent groups as such. The adoptive relationship often fell within the descent group and indicated the narrow range of property rights in the full sense. In China, Greece and India (and sometimes in Rome) the adopted son was often the paternal nephew (the brother's son) who had no automatic right of inheritance (though he might have a residual one) unless he was formally adopted; when this happened he inherited from his uncle, continued his direct line and worshipped at his ancestral shrine. He acquired the property in return for continuing another man's line, a man who might already be a member of the same descent group.

Adoption of the kind that has 'nothing to do with the welfare of children' appears to be connected with vertical as distinct from horizontal systems of inheritance; it provides a descendant, not a collateral.

Close collaterals of the same generation are never preferred heirs to the property; classificatory 'brothers' do not automatically inherit from each other, and even their sons take second place to a man's own daughters or to an adopted son. In order to turn an agnate into an heir apparent, a man adopts even his close clansman, his brother's own son. The reason for this is two-fold. First, the acceptance of the inheritance (or dowry, in the case of the appointed daughter) is linked to the acceptance of the status of descendant and dependent; it is linked to sonship. A brother cannot fulfil this role; in ancestral worship a man can sacrifice to (or otherwise propitiate) a father but not a brother; he can continue his brother's descent group but not his line of descent. To continue his line a son is needed, for this is the status with which such adoption is above all concerned. Hence the emphasis upon 'fictitious sonship'; one does not adopt brothers, but sons.

If adoption were mainly a way of increasing the kin group as such, a man would be unable to use an agnate for the purpose; the fact that he can do so stresses the limited degree of corporateness of the groups Maine defined as agnatic corporations.[25]

Both the extent and the limitations of the corporate identity are illustrated in Roman law; when a man had no *sui heredes* (sons or daughters by birth or adoption) and made no will, the nearest agnate inherited; but he never became *heres*, the heir. Maine regarded both the will and adoption (when he thought of this in terms of inheritance) as ways of alienating property from the agnates, and implied, again, that there had been a change from 'pure agnation'. If this was so, the changes that he and others have suggested took place long before any evidence existed, and the suggestions put forward concerning a development from bride-purchase to dowry, joint estates to nuclear families, pure agnation (preceded perhaps by matriliny) to adulterated descent, all lie in a highly speculative realm. What 'evidence' there is fits more easily into alternative explanations; even in the oldest comprehensive code of Eurasia, the Babylonian laws, features such as adoption and dowry are part of the legal norms.

In wishing to modify Maine's thesis, on this and other issues, I do not intend to place all the emphasis upon adoption as a means of providing an heir to a man's estate: for the property usually fell to the agnates in the absence of 'issue' (or testament). But property was deliberately used to provide an heir, a fictional son, to continue the line, with all the mystical implications this had, in ancestor-worship and for more general beliefs.

The point is best made in contrast to the general African situation, but before looking at this, I would like to consider some functional alternatives to adoption (type ii), what one might call the parent-oriented form as well as the means that traditional Eurasian societies have of coping with orphaned and destitute children, that is, the alternatives to adoption of type i (what one might call the child-oriented form).

Alternatives to adoption

The adoption of both males and females is often, for the adoptee, a means of attaining a higher social position or (at least) greater wealth;[26] one sells one's birthright, or that of one's child, for better prospects in this world. As far as the adoption of males is concerned, the institution is the functional equivalent of the 'appointed daughter', the epiclerate, the heiress, who in the absence of brothers is chosen to make a filiacentric (or paternally oriented) union and so produce an heir for her father.[27] In addition there are of course other mechanisms for getting heirs and descendants through wives rather than through daughters. Even in some monogamous societies a man may divorce a barren wife or alternatively (as we have seen occurred in China) he may take a concubine where her children were potential heirs.

There are then two widespread alternatives to adoption, namely, breeding through the appointed daughter and replacing one's wife by another spouse, a concubine or even her own handmaiden. Clearly the alternatives involving divorce or subsidiary forms of sexual union (and adoption might be a welcome possibility where these were not approved) are necessary only where one obvious 'solution' is not practised, that is, polygyny. It is significant, as we have seen, that these classical societies of Eurasia have monogamous marriage and lineal inheritance.[28] They are also highly stratified societies; with their intensive systems of agricultural production, there is considerable disparity in wealth between members of different strata; even the peasantry are firmly differentiated on the basis of land holdings. The rich have wealth to leave, even when they have no children; the less well-off can sometimes rise by making use of these mechanisms for preserving continuity (adoption, filiacentric unions and concubinage) as status-climbing devices, though the major status jumps were usually inviolate.

While adoption of my type (ii) (i.e. the provision of a childless couple with social progeny) is often practised in 'traditional' Eurasian societies, that of type (i) (i.e. the care of deprived children) is rarely found. Extended ties of kinship may have limited value for inheritance purposes where the emphasis is upon direct, lineal transmission, but such links can still provide for orphaned children; in a system of classificatory kinship (in Morgan's original sense), a man has many 'fathers'; even in the absence of such inclusive conceptual categories, provision is generally made for the orphaned children of near kin. Unwanted children of other categories can be filiated through the mother; or exposed on a hillside (though infanticide is more current in Eurasia than Africa); or again used as military recruits. In later Rome state relief and private charity alleviated the problem, partly in order to ensure a steady supply of recruits for the legions.[29]

In China, too, children were sometimes disposed of for 'economic' reasons – in this case, females. Women had to be endowed as well as raised, and infanticide saved on both accounts.[30] Control of family size, whether by infanticide, monogamy or polyandry, made it easier to retain the position of the family in the social hierarchy: too many daughters could not be endowed; too many sons could not enjoy enough land. But restrictions on family size, while often necessary to maintain the viability of families[31] in relation to their scarce productive resources, carry concomitant dangers, especially where mortality is high;[32] a man may easily find himself dropping from few heirs to none at all, and under these conditions he may well have to adopt.[33]

Fostering in Africa

In the previous sections I have contrasted the role of adoption in modern western countries with the part it plays in 'traditional' Eurasian societies. But the position in tropical Africa stood out in great contrast to both.[34] In the first place differences of status and wealth were small by comparison with Eurasia; there was little intensive agriculture; although iron was present, many 'Bronze-age' inventions were conspicuously absent, particularly writing, the wheel and the plough. Land was relatively abundant and was little improved, either by terracing or irrigation; water had to be scooped up, weights manhandled (save for donkeys in the west) and the land cultivated with the hoe. In general, land use is extensive rather than intensive and shifting agriculture still dominates the continent; soils as well as technology place limits on its productive capacity.

Under these conditions there is no great pressure to confine the transmission of basic resources within narrow limits, though regions of land shortage did exist. Brothers and nephews can inherit property, at least when there are no offspring (or sister's sons in a matrilineal system). The lineage thus provides a long series of potential heirs; in fact the whole descent group consists of intestate heirs automatically prescribed,[35] from whom property cannot be alienated by adoption, by marriage or by testament.

Adoption is therefore unnecessary for the general purpose of getting rather than begetting heirs, though there may be specific conditions under which it is found.[36] More importantly, there are other mechanisms for ensuring an adequate supply of descendants. Potential heirs are not, for example, reduced by infanticide, since there is no problem of 'providing' for one's offspring in the same way, nor (except to a limited extent) of preserving economic status through marriage or inheritance.

In the second place, monogamy is also absent and polyandrous marriages occur only in special circumstances. One does not have to restrict heirs, for an abundance of children augments rather than detracts from one's estate; people to farm are at least as important as the land to cultivate. There is no restriction on wives and a man does not even have to divorce a barren wife; he can always add to his holding. In many societies the possibility of plural marriage (apart from unions with slaves, there are no real grades of marriage such as concubinage)[37] is limited by the amount of bridewealth, so that what one saves through the sterility of the first can help to purchase an interest in the fertility of the second.[38]

Plural marriage may come about by inheriting widows as well as by direct acquisition. In the largely monogamous societies of Eurasia the inheritance of widows was usually possible only when a man had no other wives; one might then have a duty, such as Onan signally failed to fulfil, of breeding heirs to the name of a brother who had died childless. 'Go in unto thy brother's wife', he was told, 'and perform the duty of a husband's brother unto her, and raise up seed to thy brother' (Gen. 38.8). A man had to marry the widow, so that his brother's name be not blotted out of Israel (Deut. 25.5–6). But, as Patai points out, it was not simply a matter of continuing a line, for continuity also concerned the temporal estate; 'the problem of the levirate in the Bible', he writes, 'is an intricate one, interwoven as it is with regulations concerning the redemption of the landed property of a man who dies without heirs' (1959, 92). When Ruth was left a childless widow, the nearest kinsman was unable to redeem her land and marry her. So drawing off his shoe, he left her free to marry a richer and more distant relative, Boaz, who bought the land left by the father-in-law and married Ruth 'to raise up the name of the dead upon his inheritance that the name of the dead be not cut off from among his brethren and from the gate of his place' (Ruth 4.10). In Eurasia the levirate and widow inheritance, where allowed, were mainly stop-gaps, but in Africa they were practised much more extensively, providing (for certain purposes) an alternative to adoption.

In Africa the function of the levirate was not primarily to secure an heir to a man's property: an heir was already available within the descent group; in any case the property did not wait indefinitely for a proxy son.[39] Nor was it a matter of recruiting for the descent group as such, since this could be done as well by widow inheritance. But we often find the same concern as in Eurasia that a particular man should have direct descendants. In societies where ancestors are worshipped, there is clearly a premium on the continuation of a 'line of descent'; even among the Nuer, who lack ancestor worship, it is important that a man have a 'descendant' to call his name and continue his line, even if the son is born after the father has died, by a leviratic spouse or by a 'ghost wife'. The continuity of an individual's line is achieved not through adopting 'fictitious' sons (who are 'bought' with property) but by breeding sons through 'fictitious' wives acquired with bridewealth. The levirate too could be used to provide a childless brother with a son, but it was in no sense limited to this role; widows were automatically inherited, though they could often free themselves by going into 'concubinage' or by getting another man to repay the bridewealth. In any case, the institution was not just a stop-gap for childless unions.

In Africa, adoption is rare, fostering (which involves no permanent change of identity) common. When rights to specific resources are being exchanged for a birthright, then it is a permanent, not a temporary, change that has to be effected. Africa does not provide the occasion for such exchanges, and hence fostering combined with polygyny and 'corporate' inheritance can do most of the jobs done elsewhere by adoption; in particular it can take care of crisis situations by providing proxy or foster parents.[40]

Adoption in Africa today

What about the contemporary situation in Africa? Let us take the specific case of Ghana. Here the 'family' provides an heir either on a next-of-kin basis or else by selection among the eligibles.[41] Under certain conditions the testament is now used to divert property from the heir apparent and so modify, at least in particular instances, the norms of inheritance.[42] But property is rarely if ever used to acquire adopted children and continue a line. The other functions of adoption can be taken care of by fostering arrangments; among other uses, these can provide children with proxy parents and adults with proxy children, most often among their own kin.

In Ghana such arrangements persist (and perhaps increase) because the 'erosion of the family' has not reached the same proportions as in the major industrial societies, though in some groups similar problems are beginning to emerge. In the industrial sectors of European societies, the inheritance of family property is of little importance to the majority of people; at best, their direct interest in the means of production is limited to a few shares and there is no continuing concern over property to keep more than a stem family together. In this situation, training is more important than inheritance and only the very rich can use the prospect of a legacy as a bait to secure dependents. However, the lack of emphasis on kin outside one's families of birth and of marriage increases the extent of the problem of childless couples and parentless (or unwanted) children.

In Ghana, kinship continues to play an important part in the ownership and transmission of farm property, on the productive capacity of which the economy of the country largely rests. In these circumstances, fostering (especially among kin) appears to provide a more satisfactory arrangement for dealing with deprived and unwanted children since it allows of greater flexibility. In Europe there is a further consideration, for if the prospect of a more permanent identification between parent and child increases the supply of proxy-parents, this itself is an argument in its favour. But in Africa no such situation arises. 'Family' responsibility has not diminished to the point where national welfare agencies have constantly to step in. Yet in many parts there seems a danger of encouraging premature application of European models, such as attempts to protect the child by advocating extra-familial supervision and formalised procedures like adoption and institutional care as against the more flexible, kin-based practices that existed hitherto.

In Africa, wider ties of kinship are still of great importance and family responsibility is at a higher level than in industrialised countries. To introduce European procedures at this stage may retard rather than advance a country's economic growth, partly because such a step would inhibit the possible evolution of new solutions and partly because the European remedies are so costly; the job of caring for children can be done at very much less social cost by using existing conjugal units rather than by organising special custodial arrangements. The expense of social services must be prevented from swallowing up all the results of increased productivity, especially when the proposed changes are not necessarily any improvement on what was there before. In these circumstances (perhaps in most) the care of kin remains the best way of dealing with deprived children, who need the prolonged attention of foster-parents rather than public 'homes' or formal adoption. In this chapter, I have tried to point to some of the reasons why the Eurasian institution of adoption (despite the use of the term by many observers) is not widely found in Africa. This distribution is related to the way in which property is transmitted from one generation to the next by vertical inheritance. When this occurs, adoption is often used to provide an heir for a man's name and often his worship. In the African case, where the productive system makes less intensive use of land and there is less to leave in terms of restricted resources, property is less problematic and may pass through brothers to nephews; meanwhile personal continuity is often maintained through taking on wives rather than children.[43]

In the following chapter I extend the discussion from the analysis of roles to that of strategies, to the way these relationships are adopted and adapted to meet the demands of specific individuals in specific social and historical situations.

7. Strategies of heirship

The prologue to the great Chinese autobiographical novel of the eighteenth century, *Dream of the Red Chamber*, contains the following passage, in which the author sets the scene for his story:

Chen Shih-Ying was without aspirations to fame or fortune. He devoted his time to planting bamboo and watering flowers and sipping wine and writing poems. He led an idyllic life. Unfortunately he lacked one thing to complete his happiness: he was over half a hundred years of age and had no son. Only a three-year-old daughter named Lotus filled his bosom (Ts'ao, 1958, 9).

The situation confronting Chen Shih-Ying is one that is consciously faced by men and women in all human groups. But it is one whose resolution differs depending upon the alternatives available in particular societies and upon the position in the life-cycle in which an individual stands. In this chapter I want to lay out the possible mechanisms from which societies can select to deal with the problem of heirship, especially as it concerns the absence of sons, the substitutability of daughters and the excess of heirs. Though the situation covers more than the ownership and transmission of property, I shall be mainly concerned with this material aspect of heirship, especially as we have seen that the transfer of productive resources is connected with differences in the systems of social roles found in the major African and Eurasian societies.

The main problem is this. If social replacement, for whatever purpose, is carried out in a lateral direction, there is no theoretical difficulty about finding an heir; you search sideways until you find a candidate that fills the empty box. With vertical inheritance, the problem is more complex. By vertical inheritance, I mean those systems that first seek an heir in the next descending generation, i.e. among a person's children (or in matrilineal cases, his sister's children). It is more complex partly because of the simple fact that not every couple produces children and, even when they do so, their offspring may consist only of daughters or only of sons. Moreover, with vertical transmission, individuals may influence the course of events in a more direct way, for example, by pursuing a strategy of maximising their holding of children (whether these are defined biologically or not). If there are no children, then collaterals may become residual heirs. But in many of the major societies of the Eurasian continent, such a step is not regarded as an automatic one.

I start from the assumption that, in vertical systems of transmission, heirs are deliberately sought after: not just as general recruits to the lineage, clan or tribe, but as specific heirs that individuals require to secure their own particular line by acquiring descendants, preferably of their own flesh and blood.

This question of 'security' has several facets. There is the security in old age, which is a prime consideration when there are no alternative means of saving up for the period when an individual can no longer support himself directly out of his productive activities; in these situations an important part of one's savings, one's capital, consists of one's kin. Then there is the security that is gained by making provision for the continuity of the family estate, however large or small. And, related to this latter, is the security not for old age, but for the after-life, the continuity of one's name, one's memory, or one's worship.

It is not easy for individuals in advanced industrial economies to understand the importance of such security in other societies and in other sectors, when only 10 per cent of the population are engaged in primary production (that is, in directly producing what we need by way of food),[1] when they are cushioned against the uncertainties of the food-quest by national institutions, and when the ownership of the means of primary production does not have the same significance as in pre-industrial societies.

Even when the importance of having an heir is appreciated, the extent of the problem of heirlessness is rarely understood. One kinship model often employed by actors and observers alike, namely, the segmentary lineage, shows a proliferation of children to each individual member; at the very least this model assumes continuity, but often it allows for a bifurcation of males at each generation, in other words for a continuous population explosion. Indeed, there are specific reasons why such continuity should be stressed on a 'political' level, that is, at levels beyond the usual five-generational framework of the developmental cycle, grandparent to grandchild.[2]

On the 'domestic' level the situation is very different. In his discussion of the 'family cycle' in India, Collver notes that 'despite the high rate of reproduction, 22 per cent of all parents reach the end of the reproductive period without a living son. About 30 per cent have only one son living and less than half experience the security of having two or more sons' (1963, 95–6). Collver argues that this lack of security means that 'the degree of independence enjoyed by the nuclear family in America would be out of the question in rural India' (96).[3] India is a country with rapid population growth; earlier, higher mortality would have meant that the problem of male continuity would be raised in approximately 40 per cent of the cases of married couples, some half of which would have no heirs at all. With a smaller family size, the number of heirless families increases, as is seen in the model presented in Appendix 2. Records of the European nobility show that 15 per cent of married men were childless;[4] for ducal families in Britain, Hollingsworth (1964–5, 371) gives the figures shown in Table 25. If we take all marriages, then the figures for the earlier period are 27 per cent for men and 23 per cent for women.

TABLE 25   *Childlessness in marriages of completed fertility*

Cohort born	1330–1729	1730–1829	1830–1934
Males	16%	20%	20%
Females	17%	18%	13%

In pre-industrial societies, which are marked by high fertility and high mortality, the obverse of the problem of heirship is that of widowhood (or, more generally, the loss of a spouse) and of orphanhood (or the loss of a parental figure); both these problems are more severe than they are in industrial countries. Clearly one function of extended kinship ties is to cater for the dissolution of the conjugal or parental unit through death, by looking after the wives (e.g. by inheritance or the levirate) and the children (e.g. by pro-parenthood) of dead relatives.

Lateral inheritance

The provision of an heir to one's property or position, and of a support to one's old age, can be dealt with by lateral inheritance, that is, by the system that gives preference to brothers (including classificatory ones) before sons (or sisters' sons). And it can be dealt with even in lineal systems by making collaterals act automatically as residual heirs, in the absence of direct ones. In Africa, brothers were often primary heirs and almost invariably residual ones; males inherited from males and females from females; and whether inheritance was vertical or lateral, distant males were preferred to closer females. Especially in West Africa, brothers were often preferred to sons or to sisters' sons. These conditions encourage (or are encouraged by) a system of joint exploitation of land by siblings, which is more common with extensive than with intensive agriculture; farm families therefore tend to be somewhat larger.[5] But the difference is not great, since only in a limited number of families will two brothers survive their father; in less than 30 per cent of the cases where there is a one-third chance of a child surviving his father, and only in some 21 per cent if this role is restricted to a full sibling, will a brother be available to follow a brother. Such a definition is rarely true of patrilineal societies; descendants of the same agnatic grandfather are often eligible. But in matrilineal societies, lateral inheritance is sometimes limited to the offspring of one womb, after which the property drops a generation to the sister's son. Assuming a rough similarity in the fertility and mortality rates for pre-industrial societies, i.e. high fertility and high mortality, we can reckon that where the preferred heir is a lineal descendant (and where male inheritance is the rule), property will pass to collaterals at death in about two-fifths of the cases. Even where daughters are possible heirs, a sixth of the population will have to be succeeded by collaterals, unless alternative arrangements have been made.

Lineal inheritance

But whereas lateral inheritance is quite common in Africa (as is lateral succession to office), Eurasia is marked by vertical (or lineal) inheritance and succession. In terms of the transmission of property (inheritance) and office (succession), collaterals are usually set aside as residual heirs or are even eliminated altogether, a fact which is bound to affect the nature of dynasties on the one hand and of descent groups on the other.[6] This process of sloughing creates certain problems for vertical inheritance, because it means there is a possibility of having either no heir or else an heir too young to act (a situation which leads to a minority and a regency, with all the inherent dangers). Nevertheless this same process is intrinsic to the system since one of the functions of lineal succession is often the preservation of the status of offspring in a society with differentiated strata based on property-holding (or other relatively exclusive rights).

In many Eurasian societies vertical inheritance is associated with the passing of property to children not just of one but of both sexes, for it is the status of daughters as well as sons that has to be preserved. In other words, where we find 'diverging devolution', vertical inheritance is combined with the non-sexlinked transfer of property; the heritage goes downwards to children of both sexes, enabling them to maintain their status in societies where social positions depend to a significant degree on the ownership of property.

Since lateral inheritance usually provides a string of heirs, strategies of heirships are of less concern. The particular situation I want to discuss here is the failure of vertical inheritance, especially from the man's point of view. For example, what happens when a wife fails to produce a son and the husband does not wish the property to pass to collaterals by 'intestate succession'? What strategy will he adopt?

In trying to answer this question I want first to sketch the various alternatives available. Societies make use of different selections of these and individuals make use of different alternatives within the spectrum available to the particular society. I shall attempt to specify some of the reasons for selecting one as against another. Clearly the individual's choice will depend upon his position in the life-cycle. He may realise that his wife is barren within a few years of marriage and his subsequent actions may flow from this fact. On the other hand, if she is fertile, he will realise that she has produced no son (as distinct from daughters) only when she stops childbearing; indeed the search for a son will tend to increase his holding of girls. And he will realise he has no surviving heir only on his deathbed. At each of these points in the developmental cycle, different strategies will be appropriate.

Before analysing the possible alternatives, a further fact needs to be borne in mind. One means of hedging against the failure of the male line is to produce more than one son. But in systems of partible inheritance, this sort of security is bought at the expense of dividing the property.[7] For the better-off, potential division may be the lesser of two evils; but for the poor, it could be disastrous. Hence at the lower end of the hierarchy, there is a knife-edge between having too few heirs for comfort and producing too many claimants for restricted resources. The delicate relationship between land, dowry and strategy of heirship has been very clearly put by J.-L. Flandrin in his volume on *Les Amours paysannes (XVIᵉ–XIXᵉ siècle)*.

Le problème de dot, le plus voyant, s'incrivait dans une ensemble plus vaste de contraintes économiques qu'il importe d'analyser. Dans une vielle société rurale où toute la terre arable était appropriée, il était essentiel pour chaque famille de conserver intact son patrimoine foncier. Pour les unes c'était le principal garant de leur place dans la hiérarchie sociale; pour les plus pauvres, c'était leur moyen de subsistance. Or à chaque échelon de la pyramid sociale la prolificité des familles risquait d'entraîner un morcellement de ce patrimoine. Nombres des contraintes qui pesaient sur le mariage avaient fin de parer à ce risqu' (1975: 62).

The problems of over- and under-production of heirs are closely interrelated, but it is the latter with which I am mainly concerned.

Adding wives

An heirless man can provide himself with an heir either indirectly, by adding wives, or directly, by adding children. Should he adopt the first of these alternatives, he increases his holding of spouses to be in a better position to have an heir. However, as I have argued earlier, polygyny presents difficulties for systems of diverging devolution (a form of vertical inheritance), where the conjugal group has been established on a property-holding basis.[8] It is not surprising to find, therefore, that the major Eurasian societies have definite tendencies towards monogamy. Even where this form of marriage is not the only institutionalised type, the exceptions are very often concerned specifically with the production of heirs; where plural unions are allowed, second marriages are likely to be placed in a distinct category, as is the case with concubines in China or hand-maidens and second wives in Israel (in the marriage of Jacob, for example); unlike first marriages, they are usually unendowed, without property but for continuity. Here the second union, not polygyny but concubinage, is used to produce heirs. Where this is so, it is clear the offspring of such a union must carry full rights of inheritance, otherwise the institution would fail in one of its main purposes. In this respect there is an interesting contrast with certain types of 'lesser' marriage which deliberately exclude a child of the offspring of the union from inheriting the position of the father. I am thinking not only of situations where a man takes a mistress (that is, a relatively permanent sexual partner who has no conjugal rights) and hence excludes the 'natural' issue of the union from rights to his property, with the effect that we see in *King Lear* upon the relationship between Edmund, Edgar and their father. But the same situation also occurs with regard to morganatic marriages; such a union, which does carry certain conjugal rights, specifically excludes the offspring from succeeding to the position of the father, and for this reason it was suggested as the solution to the liaison between the Duke of Windsor (then King of England) and Mrs Simpson. It is a mechanism of discontinuity rather than of continuity. A woman is taken for her sexual and domestic services, not for her property, nor for her heir-producing powers. In this context, it is useful to make an analytical distinction between the quasi-conjugal statuses of concubine, mistress and morganatic spouse, based upon the presence or absence of certain rights involved in a 'full' marriage.

Thirdly, in addition to plural marriage and concubinage, we have the strategy of divorce and remarriage, the strategy adopted by the Shah of Persia when he dismissed his Queen Soraya, and pursued by Henry VIII in his treatment of his unproductive spouses. Under this serial monogamy, a man can divorce an existing wife in order to try again with a second spouse. Clearly the later he marries, the less chance he has of proving a woman's fertility and of finding another if she is deficient. Of course, testing may occur before marriage and the desire for certainty might have accounted for part of the large percentage of births in certain English counties that occurred within the first nine months of marriage.[9] But this practice is likely to be less important the greater the property involved, since in these cases a specific marriage contract is required in order to clinch the union and the sexuality of women comes under tighter control.

A variant upon the theme of serial monogamy through divorce is the remarriage of a widower to a fertile spouse; the remarriage of a widow is of somewhat less significance for the problem of heirship, unless she is obligated (as in the Jewish levirate) to produce a child to her dead husband's name.[10] Where these practices are allowed, the production of a man's heirs extends beyond the fertile period of a particular married couple.

However, a plurality of marriages, whether embarked upon serially or contemporaneously, is likely to create problems for the unions established on the basis of a property-match. In Arab societies, high divorce and diverging devolution go together; according to the *United Nations Demographic Yearbook* (1969), the divorce rate in Egypt was 12.9 per thousand for 1968.[11] But the main form that diverging devolution takes in these countries is the inheritance by women of a share of their paternal property. It is rather dowry (i.e. transfer at the time of marriage) that one would specifically associate with restrictions on polygyny, divorce and remarriage, for it is this transaction that would tend to complicate the dissolution of a conjugal union.

Clearly, the divorce of a wife in order to secure an heir by a second spouse is unnecessary where polygyny or concubinage is allowed, since one can simply add to one's holding of women without having to discard any of the existing complement; in Africa the barren woman may want to change husbands, but husbands rarely divorce barren women.[12] In Eurasia, divorce followed by remarriage is a feasible strategy for obtaining an heir, but it brings its own complications; for when marriage establishes a conjugal fund by means of dowry, then dissolution of the union involves a dismantling of the fund, a procedure which may involve great difficulties depending on the size and nature of the property.

Add children

We see, then, that in Africa polygyny is the main device for producing a specific heir (where one is required). In addition, the responsibility for providing continuity at a man's death may extend to his brother, who has the obligation to produce children to the dead man's name either by the levirate or else by ghost marriage.[13]

In Eurasia, however, the alternative procedure is favoured, namely an increase at the junior rather than at the senior generation. Substitute filiation is found more frequently than substitute marriage; a man provides himself with an additional child rather than an additional wife. What are the various ways in which he can do this? The first possibility is to substitute a daughter for a son. Let us assume that any child will have a one-third chance of outliving its father, a reasonable assumption for pre-industrial societies. On the basis of a completed family size of 6.0, 38 per cent of the owners of farms (or 'agricultural holdings') in any community will have no son to inherit (Appendix 2). Some 21 per cent of the total number of families will have a daughter who could take over the property. However, in 17 per cent of the cases, there will be no available offspring at all and some other mechanism of continuity must be brought into play. The percentages listed above will vary with the demographic parameters. Late marriage will produce fewer legitimate male heirs. A greater sex

lifferential in age at marriage will of itself produce a greater turnover of
spouses,[14] the effects of which will vary with the inheritance system. But a
large differential in favour of women will mean that there will also be a large
number of widows. If they have use of conjugal property until death, then
again more parents are likely to be without heirs, more daughters are likely to
inherit, and an increased proportion of property will be effectively under the
control of women[15] or available for redistribution outside the family. These
figures could be important for the build-up of church lands, since the greater
number of heirless laymen, the greater the possible benefits to the clergy.[16]

The figure given by Collver of 6.1 for completed family size for his contemporary Indian data is virtually the same as in England and Wales for those
women married between 1861–9, another period of population growth: the
average was 6.16 (Wrigley, 1969: 196). After 1870 the decline in family size
was very rapid[17] (Wrigley, 1969: Table 5.17) until it reached 2.04 for the
cohort married in 1935–9. The implications with regard to male heirs were
radical; with smaller family size, a smaller proportion of property would be
inherited by sons.

In the absence of male offspring, we have two different strategies, depending upon whether preference in inheritance is given to close women before
more distant males, as seems to be the case in much of the Eurasian continent
and is, I have argued, related to the type of socio-economic system. If this
option is open, one would expect to find a considerable degree of uxorilocal
marriage taking place in communities where landed property was of major
significance. Those younger brothers who have been unable to acquire a farm
of their own are likely to marry heiresses.[18]

In farming societies where land is short, inheriting daughters are clearly
attractive brides; for them and their lands men will 'marry in' or as the French
say, 'faire le gendre'. Although the main rule for post-marital residence is for
the wife to join the husband, in this situation the reverse will occur. Where
women change their name at marriage, documentary records will appear to
show a new family taking over, whereas in fact continuity has been maintained
through the daughter. The extent of this type of alternative marriage will vary
with the size of the family; the lower the size, the greater the likelihood of such
unions.

In a recent survey of Finnish farms, it was found that of 96 holdings con-
taining married couples and older parents, the proportion of husband's parents
was 66 per cent and of wife's parents 34 per cent.[19] The author's hypothesis is
that the proportion of in-marrying sons-in-law has increased due to the migration of males into towns (Sweetser, 1964, 222). Such a change could also be
affected by a decrease in family size, which automatically increases the percentage of households without a male heir. However the effect on the percent-

age of families with only female offspring is relatively small under situations
with the least favourable mortality (i.e. over 50 per cent chance of a child dying
before his father); it is the number of heirless families that increases rapidly as
the mean family size (i.e. number of children) falls to the modern Western
figure. Though the difference in 'girls only' is clearly less important as mortality
improves, it is still significant. At the 35 per cent level, the percentage of families with only girls varies from 12.2 with a mean family size of 6, to 24.7 with a
family size of 2.5, while the corresponding figures for childless families (i.e.
those without male or female heirs) are 2.0 and 19.7. Hence the unadjusted
percentage of families without any male heirs increases from 14.2 to 44.4. With
a large differential in the age of marriage and with a system whereby parental
property passes between spouses before it goes to children, then the decrease in
family size will mean an increase in the number of heirless ('merry') widows.
Whatever the reasons, the recent Finnish figures point to the potential size of
the problem; uxorilocal marriages accounted for one third of the total number
of 'extended' families.

When great emphasis is placed upon the continuity of the name or named
descent line, then this form of alternative marriage (often lower in status than
where the woman moves to the man) may carry the further implication either
of a change of the man's name or (where unilineal descent groups are found)
of the man producing for his wife's clan or lineage, as in the Chinese case
described by Hsu (1949, 102).

Thus the epiclerate (the institution of the inheriting daughter) is often
associated with the filiacentric union (where a man makes an uxorilocal marriage
in a predominantly virilocal system of postmarital residence) and less frequently
with the institution whereby the husband begets children for his wife's kin.
The 'appointed daughter' acts as a social male, producing children for her own
natal group.[20] The incoming son-in-law on the other hand acts like an adopted
child, since in return for enjoying the property (if only the interest or usu-
fruct), he looks after not only his wife but her surviving parents as well; clearly
this role is more attractive where a woman 'inherits' at marriage by way of the
dowry, rather than at the death of her parents.

With a stable population, it would be possible to re-allocate all but a small
percentage of farms at each generation by means of such filiacentric unions,
without anybody having to escape to the towns or to leave the community in
any other way. The transmission of the remaining farms where no offspring
exists calls for an additional strategy, that is, the importation of a male heir
from 'outside'. The rule of inheritance may allow for the resort to collaterals.
But in many parts of Europe and Asia, collaterals were not automatically heirs.
As we have seen, in China as in Greece, an agnate had to be specifically adopted,
turned ritually into the son of the holder, before he could inherit, even if he

was a member of one and the same clan. The adoption of the father's brother's son was a feature of heirless families in ancient Greece, and even where a daughter was the heir (*epikleros*), this relative was seen as the preferred husband/son. If women are prevented from acting as heirs, then adoption may be used more frequently; in the instance we employed earlier, where women did inherit, one could expect heirs to be adopted in a maximum of 17 per cent of the cases. The adoptees could of course be either outsiders or kinsmen; but in any case the major function is clear: until the present century, the heir-producing aspects of adoption showed a straight ascendancy over the child-welfare ones.[21]

In Africa, the use of a daughter, not as heir but to produce sons for her lineage, does occur (e.g. in Dahomey, Banyoro, and among the LoDagaa), but the practice takes on a different slant since rarely do women control property inherited from males; they simply produce the heirs. Adoption on the other hand is scarcely known, at least in the Eurasian sense, even though fostering is common.[22]

Subtracting children

But the security of one's life is not simply a matter of obtaining heirs, regardless of numbers, but also of balancing property against people; it is a question of the viability of the estate.[23] If land is scarce, and if a man has only enough to support one elementary family, then he has to control either the number of heirs he produces (usually his sons), or else their subsequent employment. These considerations will clearly affect the poor more than the rich; hence the widespread tendency, noted in China (Freedman, 1970, 3), for 'stem families' to be found among the poor, and 'extended families' among the rich.[24] One can reduce the number of heirs in a variety of ways:

1 By contraceptive techniques, that is, by preventing the birth of additional children beyond those required for continuity.

2 By abortion and infanticide, that is, by eliminating those who have already been conceived or born. An extension of this strategy is the bastardisation of children at an even later stage in the life-cycle, a point that bears upon the difference between Africa and Eurasia regarding the concept of legitimacy.

3 By reducing the claim of additional sons and daughters upon the estate, which itself may take a variety of forms:

    (a) The reduction of the claims of other children can be done on the spot, by maintaining only unmarried sons and daughters out of the estate, other than the heir himself (e.g. Ireland, Arensberg and Kimball, 1940; Medieval England, Homans, 1941; Tibet, Carrasco, 1959).

(b)   The surplus children may go into service, not permanently but for part of the developmental cycle. This situation perhaps accounts for the high percentages of servants in some Eurasian societies, at many different levels of the social system (e.g. in England, Laslett, 1969, 219).[25]

(c)   A further alternative is emigration to the towns or a less permanent absence in the army (which itself often encourages celibacy on organisational grounds); this solution adds up to the provision of some alternative employment.

(d)   Finally there is the church, which often encourages asceticism in the form of celibacy (e.g., Tibet and various Christian denominations).

The techniques of birth control to which I have referred apply only to the post-heir producing stage, when the problem of heirship has already been settled. In societies that prefer a male heir, it is likely that the tendency to family limitation (which will manifest itself only in a certain proportion of families) will appear after the birth of the second male, though when infant mortality drops, the first male may be considered sufficient. Since these strategies of parenthood will be much influenced by present circumstances, by family history and by ideology (which often pulls in one direction and pushes in another), there will be great individual variation. Nevertheless the sibling group seems more likely to end with a male.[26]

Discussing Finnish data studied by Renkonen, Edwards notes that in two-child families the arrangement FM seems particularly popular, and this is also true in the case of the last two children in families of three, where the proportion continuing procreation is least for the FFM combination; the most likely to continue are those with MFF and FFF sequences. According to Edwards (1966), in so far as the decision to continue a three-child family is based on sex sequences, it seems to depend on the sex of the last two.[27] The differences are not great, though they are significant; they seem likely to have greater significance for peasant populations than for urban ones;[28] rural families are more concerned with the transmission of the means of production from one generation to the next, while urban ones seem more likely to aim for a balance between the sexes. Among completed two-child families listed in *Who's Who in America*, there is a striking excess of male–female sets, i.e. MF or FM (Fancher, 1956), a distribution representing a deliberate desire for balance (Gittelsohn, 1960).

Strategies of heirship are also likely to influence the age of marriage and will therefore be related to rates of widowhood, divorce and orphanhood. But these features require explanation in further depth; here I am mainly concerned with the problem of heirship itself.

Conclusions

n Chapter 5 we discussed two different kinds of role system found in Africa
and Eurasia, or rather under African hoe culture and Eurasian plough farm-
ng. These differences are related to the high productivity of the plough, the
specialisation that this permits, the scarcity of land which it creates or aggra-
vates, and the differential holdings of land and of capital which then become
important. In Africa on the other hand, productivity was low and there was
little full-time specialisation; most craftsmen were also farmers, even when
assisted by slaves. Land as distinct from labour was rarely a scarce resource
and hence its exclusive ownership was not the basis of social stratification,
either locally or nationally.

The different use made of strategies of heirship in Africa and Eurasia seems
to be related to this major fact. In Africa personal continuity was important
but there was less pressure to provide a direct heir to a specific estate, since
economic differentiation was small and there was little overall shortage of the
basic means of production, namely, land. Moreover, the marriage of daughters
had little effect on their socio-economic position, so that they did not need to
be endowed by their parents. In Eurasia, on the other hand, the problem of
heirship was raised in a much more critical way because socio-economic status
was at stake; a man not only aimed to provide for his offspring (male and
female) in order that they should not fall in the social hierarchy, but he was
also concerned with the problem of old age and with the future of the estate;
hence the search for a substitute heir, even a son-in-law, when he did not have
an heir to his body.

In examining the relationship of the system of inheritance to other institutions such as marriage and adoption, as well as variables such as family size or
rates of divorce, we are faced with a range of possibilities open to human societies, with a set of alternatives available to the members of a particular society,
and finally with the strategies employed by individuals in selecting among these
alternatives. The dividing lines between these categories are not hard and fast;
individual choice and structural alternative coexist in the same field. For
example, new demographic conditions, such as the loss of men in war, may lead
people to adopt new strategies and hence extend, perhaps permanently, the
alternatives available to them. There is a great danger in the social sciences of
seeing 'ideal and actual' behaviour, 'belief and action', normative and statistical
models, as too distinct one from another. Such an approach fails to allow
sufficiently for internally generated social change, or indeed for the range of
individual behaviour; it regards 'norms' as of the same order of reality as a
template. I have tried to spell out the various possibilities, to link the selection
among them with other features of social organisation, and finally to suggest

some of the factors behind the individual choice of alternatives at specific phases of the life-cycle, especially as they relate to the composition of one's family and the distribution of one's property. These alternatives comprise the strategies of heirship for individuals and for societies, but they may also vary according to the particular social group within a society to which an individual belongs. In the next chapter we consider the relationship of these variables to the nature of the hierarchical group to which individuals belong, that is, to the existence of social classes.

8. Class and marriage

The distribution of variables such as diverging devolution and in-marriage tends to be linked (theoretically and empirically, logically and statistically, I argue) to Africa on the one hand and the major Eurasian civilisations on the other. So too does the distribution of roles such as that of concubine and co-wife, of mechanisms such as adoption and of various other strategies of heirship. In this chapter, I examine the way these features are related to types of 'class', to modes of social stratification, that once again set Africa apart from the states of Europe and Asia.

A problem about West Africa was raised a hundred years ago by Richard Burton in the description of his mission to Gelele, king of the state of Dahomey. 'Truly it is said that whilst the poor man in the North is the son of a pauper, the poor man in the Tropics is the son of a prince' (1864, 40–1). It is a problem that was taken up fifty years later in another form by the Gold Coast lawyer from Cape Coast, John Mensah Sarbah, when he wrote that 'in the African social system the formation of a pauper class is unknown, nor is there antagonism of class against class' (Redwar, 1909; vi). And it is a problem that has been central to current controversies between European Marxists on the one hand, and African socialists on the other, about the nature of the systems of stratification in that continent (Grundy, 1964).

Each of these statements involves some contrast, implicit or explicit, between the class structure of African and Eurasian states, if one understands the North (in Burton's characteristic aphorism) to mean Eurasia and the South, Africa. It is the implications for the comparative analysis of stratification, or more specifically for status groups, that I want to pursue by considering the relationship between class and marriage.

Class

In all the major continents of the world, the more technologically advanced societies are marked by their unequal distribution of power and status. It is this power bank, Parsons suggests, that among other things, provides the mechanism for the mobilisation of resources in the interest of the collective action needed for the running of complex societies (1964, 51). The terms we use to analyse the major groups in this wide range of stratified systems, in whatever part of the world they are found, derive directly from the Eurasian experience. Three main concepts are employed: class, as typified by the modern Western world; caste, characteristic of India; and the estates (or *Stände*) of feudal Europe. In sociological discussions the major difference between class and caste turns upon the openness or closure of a series of horizontally juxta-posed groups or strata, that is, upon whether or not mobility is allowed between them.[1]

In visual terms, such systems are often diagrammed as a kind of layer cake, one element spread on top of the next like a series of deposits in a well-conducted archaeological dig, the different units being arranged in a single hierarchy in which each group is defined as being above, below, or in-between. Or alter-natively, to use another culinary metaphor, as a jam sandwich, with most of the jam at the top.

I am concerned with these models, verbal and visual, because they may lead us to neglect certain basic differences between such groups as they are found in the major societies of Eurasia (which are in some ways closer together than the categorisation allows) and in the state systems of Africa (which in certain respects stand opposed both to class and caste). This is not simply a matter of setting right the historical record. A good deal more is at stake. From the standpoint of social theory, the adoption of a particular model affects the categories and measures of sociological inquiry. From the standpoint of social practice, it affects (or could affect) social policy in developing and developed nations alike. At the very least, it influences one's understanding of the role of the new elites.[2]

First of all, analytic categories of this degree of abstraction are of limited use for many, possibly most, scientific purposes. The very fact that they are drained of content, of 'culture', to such an extent has obscured the important differences. For example, the term 'feudal' has frequently been applied both to medieval Europe and to pre-colonial Africa, giving insufficient attention to differences in the economy as well as in other spheres.[3]

But, with regard to status groups, there are more specific reasons why these general concepts have given rise to misunderstanding. Clearly, pre-colonial African states had no caste system (though some had castes); neither did they have classes in the modern European sense, if mobility is to be counted as a central feature.[4] How is their type of status group best described? In his excellent account of the Nupe of Nigeria, Nadel concludes that this state is above all a class system (1942, 127–35). However, this study, which is significantly entitled *A Black Byzantium*, is replete with feudal comparisons, implicit as well as explicit. This would suggest that the model of *Stände* might be more appropriate. Many other authors have pursued this feudal analogy, accepting the built-in assumption that these units were of a type found in Europe at an earlier date. I want to suggest that even if we are forced to use such terms because of the poverty of our analytical vocabulary and a natural reluctance to proliferate neologisms, we should bear in mind the basic differences between status groups in the two continental areas and beware of general statements based (often unconsciously) upon the Eurasian experience alone.

Let us examine a particular case where this difference has been overlooked. In most discussions, classes, castes and estates are seen as having certain basic features in common. One widespread idea is that the social distance between classes is maintained by various blocks in the system of intergroup communication, that is, by restrictions upon marrying out, upon eating together, and upon other forms of social intercourse. While these restrictions do not always have the obligatory character found in caste hierarchies, and while formal freedom often exists, they are still effective in maintaining and building barriers between the status groups in a particular society.

Clearly the most effective such barrier is that on intermarriage, since such a tie would bring the two groups into close conjugal, affinal, and more general social relationships. It is therefore upon the marital arrangements between the different strata that I first want to concentrate.

Marriage

In sociological writings, there is a widely held belief that all status groups discourage intermarriage. This idea exists even among those writers who display an intelligent appreciation of cross-cultural analysis. In his work on social stratification, Bernard Barber claims that 'all societies tend to disapprove not only of all marriage between people from different social classes but also of all social relations between them that could lead to marriage' (1957, 123). Even in a relatively open-class society like the United States, marriage within the social class prevails. According to Hollingshead, 83 per cent of all New Haven marriages were between people who had been living in neighbourhoods of the same or adjacent social class positions (1950, 625).[5]

Some years earlier, Kingsley Davis presented a theoretical paper discussing why this should be so. He maintained that 'a cardinal principle of every stratified social order is that the majority of those marrying shall marry equals'; endogamy, or at least preferential in-marriage, is the rule of class, caste and *Stände*. The reason, he claims, is that marriage implies equality. 'If some persons are "untouchable," they must also be unmarriageable, and if food

which they cook is "uneatable" they must also be "unusable" in the kitchen.'
He goes on to say that 'a wife reared in a social stratum widely different from
her husband's is apt to inculcate ideas and behavior incompatible with the
position the children will inherit from their father, thus creating a hiatus
between their status and their role' (1941, 337–8). In other words, intermarriage would make it impossible to maintain extensive differences in behaviour between individuals and groups, since it would lead to a merging of the
subcultures that distinguish them.

In another contribution to the subject published in the same year, Robert
Merton stresses the same point, though in a somewhat wider social context.
'Intermarriage between persons of radically different social status thus con-
flicts with the existing organization of cliques and friendship groups involving
the spouses and their kin. Rules of avoidance or social distance and rules of
accessibility are brought into open conflict' (1964 [1941], 142). Merton's discussion deals mainly with ethnic caste, since he is trying to account for the predominance, among black–white marriages in the United States, of unions
between male blacks and female whites. But the wider concern is with the close
relationship between marriage policy and stratification.

As far as this particular situation goes, the general argument is a sound one.
But it is not in fact the case that all stratified systems demand a high degree of
in-marriage. As we have seen, status endogamy and related forms of in-
marriage are certainly characteristic of the major Eurasian societies. In Africa,
on the other hand, endogamy is rarely found except in ethnic situations, in
particular those where ruling groups of northern origin have established themselves over black agriculturalists, as happened in South Africa, Ethiopia, the
East African coast, certain Interlacustrine states, and on the Saharan fringe
(e.g. in Timbuktu). In the major states of West Africa, ruling groups were
rarely if ever endogamous. Indeed, where the ruling dynasty consisted of an
exogamous clan or lineage, both male and female members were obliged to take
their spouses from outside the ruling group; *conubium* was not merely formally
open, as in a class system, but obligatorily so. However, even where the ruling
group does not consist of a single exogamous clan, intermarriage is widespread.
Take the kingdom of Gonja in northern Ghana.[6] Originally a conquest state
established by Mande horsemen in the seventeenth century, it comprises four
major socio-political categories, the ruling Gbanya (who claim agnatic descent
from the leader of the conquest), the Muslims (who mainly descend from those
attached to the ruling house), the commoners (largely the descendants of
conquered autochthones and specialist service groups), and finally the slaves
(who were constantly absorbed into the commoner stratum and who were
continually recruited by raiding and purchase). In addition there was a sizable
body of strangers whose activities centred upon the great trading town of

Salaga, where forest products were exchanged for northern livestock, minerals, and manufactures. Examination of the social groups of spouses in 515 Gonja marriages[7] shows that men of all groups take a large proportion of wives from strata other than their own. This is very pronounced among Muslim men (two-thirds of whose marriages are outside the strata) and for men of the ruling group (four-fifths of whose marriages are outside). Even one-quarter of the men from the numerically dominant commoner strata married women from other groups. Much the same picture emerges from a study of the marriages of the previous generation, indicating that the situation we find in this society is not a new one. Indeed, things were probably like this from the beginning. It was presumably because of intermarriage that, as so often occurs in Africa, the ruling strata lost its original language and adopted the speech of one of the groups it had conquered. It remains true today that, while marriages of alliance are sometimes made between friends in the ruling group, many royals express a preference for the daughters of commoners, who are said to be less work-shy and more faithful than their own sisters. In the nearby kingdom of Bariba, in north Dahomey, similar preferences for 'low' marriage were openly expressed by male members of the ruling group,[8] and it was said that the princesses of the matrilineal Ashanti, through whom royal blood and claims to office were transmitted, preferred the lighter-skinned males from the North, men who could only have been strangers or slaves. Indeed, so little objection was there to 'low' marriage in that area that a Gonja prince once remarked to me that 'all our mothers were slaves'.

These systems of effectively open *conubium*, which are widespread in Africa, stand out in sharp opposition to the marriage arrangements of the major states in Eurasia, whether they are stratified by caste or by class. In these societies, like tends to marry like, or better. Fathers try to arrange the marriage of their daughters to men of equal or superior standing (i.e. hypergamy), but as a marriage policy, hypogamy is firmly discouraged and rarely promoted.[9] The result, as Tylor pointed out, is the isolation of groups.[10]

In Africa, the opposite is true. The different strata are bound together by a network of intermarriages which has the profound implications for the social system that Tylor, Davis and others have suggested. In order to indicate the effects on culture, as well as upon social integration, I take the apparently trivial example of cooking, since its association with sex and marriage is close.

Cooking

Given the practice of heterogamy (or open *conubium*), it is clearly difficult to maintain or institutionalise 'class' differences, that is, internal differences of culture other than those based upon expenditure alone. When husbands and

wives come from different groups, the women can hardly be expected to raise
children in the ways of their affines rather than their own – unless their role is
largely replaced by domestic servants of one kind or another. If societies are
polygynous as well as heterogamous, the situation becomes yet more complex.
The women living in a common household will be of different origins and their
ways of acting are likely to move towards a common mean. Indeed, there is
some evidence for the emergence of new norms out of this kind of mutual
accommodation in the multitribal dwelling groups of lower-status migrants in
West African cities, and this process is certainly reflected in their tendency to
adopt a standardised repertoire of recipes.[11] Under circumstances such as
these – the large heterogeneous dwelling, where a favourable climate allows
women and children to work mainly in the open common space of the court-
yard rather than be confined to the closed private space of the room – the
pressures are likely to be toward cultural homogeneity and political identification.

Contrast the Eurasian situation: the difference between the centralised
societies of Africa and Eurasia are highlighted in the household economy.
While Eurasia had a *haute cuisine* as well as a lower, *basse cuisine*, Africa had
neither; its cooking was demotic. Or rather, what cultural differentiation
existed did so in those societies like Ruanda, where the strata were in-marrying
and did not mix at the domestic level. Otherwise it was largely a matter of
quantitative rather than qualitative differences.

There is, of course, a danger in drawing too stark a contrast. One of the
great drawbacks of contemporary structural analysis is its devotion to crude
oppositions rather than more subtle measurements. Clearly, in the mercantile
and warrior states of West Africa, ways of acting depended upon one's social
status. Burton wrote of the king in Dahomey that he would not allow the
peasants to cultivate certain cash crops around the port of Whydah; a chief
could not alter his house without the king's permission; and so on (1864,
180–1). But such distinctions did not lie in the traditional patterns of culture;
they tended to be attached to specific roles rather than to general strata and to
derive from the authority of the king rather than from internal differentiation.
Moreover, intermarriage prevented too great a separation, too complete an
isolation, to develop between the strata. There was broad homogeneity in
marriage, cooking and other aspects of culture, even though the strata had
differential access to political office.

Implications and explanation

I have suggested that the usual way of looking at the status groups in stratified
societies takes account of too few important variables. As distinct from Eurasian

societies, most African states do not discourage marriage between status groups. On the contrary, they encourage such arrangements. The consequences are clear: groups tend to merge culturally even though they are politically distinct, and this is a fact of considerable political significance.

But why do Eurasian societies tend to isolate their classes and African societies to integrate theirs? What are the preconditions and the implications of these differences? In offering an explanation I am dealing with a trend, though one that, as we saw earlier, has statistical support at a number of points. I am not claiming to explain all the phenomena in question, but only a significant part of them; where numerical material is available, the extent of that part is shown by the coefficient of association. By drawing attention to the role of certain economic variables in Eurasian societies, I do not intend to reduce class and caste to epiphenomena of the economy. Religious and other aspects of such hierarchies exist in their own right.[12] But I am pointing to what I consider to be the necessary preconditions for the development of certain major aspects of these institutions and to the social implications of this fact.[13]

It is important to remember that the in-marrying tendency of European and Asian societies was not simply a feature of the major social categories known as castes or classes. Bloch insists that the marriages of like to like (or to above) occurred at all levels and for all roles. A serf was not allowed to marry outside the group of serfs dependent on the same lord (1966, 88). Duby quotes a medieval source as stating: 'Les hommes de la terre de Saint-Pierre ne prendront pas de femmes étrangères, tant qu'ils pourront trouver dans la cour des femmes qu'ils puissent épouser. Qu'il en soit de meme pour les femmes' (1962, 451). The 'small world of seigneurial sergeants', writes Bloch, developed a 'class solidarity' by inheritance and by in-marriage. In the twelfth and thirteenth centuries, 'the sons and daughters of bailiffs preferred to choose their marriage partners from among their opposite numbers on other *seigneuries*. When people are concerned to marry "within their own circle," there is tangible proof that the "circle" is on its way to becoming a class' (1966, 192). In the towns the same tendency occurred among merchants' daughters, even when they were orphans. A fourteenth-century record from London shows fifty-three out of sixty-three such girls (84 per cent) marrying merchants. Of the other ten, five were married to gentlemen and five to citizens of lesser companies. A yet higher proportion of widows remarried in their own sphere (Thrupp, 1948, 26). As for the great landed families, the position here is well known from the recent work of Holmes (1957) for the medieval period, of Stone (1960–1, 1967) for Tudor and Stuart England, and Habbakuk (1955b) for the eighteenth century. Habbakuk describes the attempts of the gentry to secure proper marriages for their daughters: 'The marriages between

landed families in the eighteenth century were more like treaties of alliance
between sovereign states than love matches; they involved hard bargaining in
which the size of the bride's fortune was carefully matched against the income
which the bridegroom's father was prepared to settle on him' (1955b, 158).
Similar kinds of arrangements were made at the marriages of modern Irish
peasants (Arensberg and Kimball, 1940), Greek villagers (Friedl, 1962), and in
Indian castes (Kapadia, 1966, 137). In all these cases, it is not simply a
question of the absence of marriage between the groups (though this fact is of
great significance in caste systems) but of matching like for like, or getting an
even better bargain. And the usual mechanism by which this matching is
achieved is the matching of property, often by means of the dowry, whereby
a woman acquired her portion upon marriage (or a jointure upon widowhood)
rather than at the death of her father or mother. Dowry systems, and indeed
the whole process by which property is passed to the offspring of both sexes
by diverging devolution, is characteristic of the centralised societies of
Eurasia (J. Goody, 1962, 307–20), those very societies that are also
marked by the tendency to marry-in.

The contrast between Eurasia and Africa in terms of the openness of
marriage (in-marriage and out-marriage) is paralleled by a contrast in marriage
transactions (dowry and bridewealth). In Africa there is no dowry, except in
areas directly influenced by Mediterranean practice, nor is there any transmission of property between males and females, either at death or at marriage.
What then is the connection between Eurasia, dowry, and in-marriage on the
one hand, and Africa, bridewealth, and out-marriage on the other? If we see
in-marriage and dowry as methods of preserving differences of property and
status in contrast to bridewealth and out-marriage which diffuse them, why
then should these features be associated with Eurasia rather than Africa?

In explaining the difference, I want to begin by recalling Bloch's account of
French Rural History (1966) where he traces the social developments associated
with the use of the plough and the rise of an increasingly intensive agriculture in Europe. In another outstanding study, Homans (1941) also relates
differences in social structure to differences in agricultural practice.

It is reasonable to look for similar differences in the present case. As distinct
from the major societies of Eurasia, African states have simple systems of
farming, since the continent lacks the plough, the wheel and often a good
soil. Frequently the exploitation of the land takes the form of shifting agriculture. Where population densities increase, land may be more permanently
cultivated, as in the Fra-fra region of northern Ghana, but productivity still
remains at a low level. In this particular area, Llyn (1942) found the average
area farmed per man was 2.49 acres (0.66 per person). While the cereal grown
in the small fertilised plot around the compound yielded 2,000 pounds per

acre, the yield of unmanured land dropped to one-tenth of this amount. On these yields he claimed it was difficult for a family to subsist without exchanging their livestock for the grain from less-crowded areas (1942, 78–83). The west of Ghana's Upper Region is less populated than this central part. In that area, three groups cultivated the following average acreages per person: LoWiili 0.9; LoDagaba 1.5; Dagaba 1.8. The rough acreage for an elementary family (i.e. per man) was therefore 3.6; 5; and 6.2 acres respectively. Internal variation within these groups was small. Of the three, the Dagaba had access to as much bushland as they could farm (J. Goody 1956, 30; 1958, 64); their acreage probably represents about the limit a man could cultivate by the hoe under these conditions. Consequently farmers could produce relatively little by way of surplus, at least in terms of cereal.[14] While a chief could employ the labour of freemen or slaves to work the land, it would bring him a very small reward when compared with the situation that existed under plough cultivation in medieval England and in other parts of Eurasia. Figures are difficult to come by for medieval Europe, but the details of the Glastonbury Manors are sufficiently precise to make a limited point. Here 260 holdings were half a virgate (30 acres) or more and 350 were of 5 acres or less (Postan 1950, 242). In comparing these acreages we must make allowances for differences in the farming system, since in the medieval case fallow land is included in the measurement of the holding. On the other hand, we must remember that the virgate was only a quarter of the acreage a family could, in theory, farm in one year, namely, a hide. What is remarkable, if viewed from the African standpoint, is not so much the overlap between the larger farms under hoe cultivation and the smaller farms under plough, but the immensely greater potential of plough farming and the massive inequalities of holdings in land which it allowed.

The figures I have given are for western Europe, but elsewhere, too, the animal-drawn plough meant a very significant leap forward in the productive capacity of individuals. Its critical role has been discussed by many writers. Generalists like Childe (1954a) and McNeill (1963) have stressed its role in the growth of human civilisation; more specifically, Hole and Flannery (1967) have argued for a close relationship between the nature of the productive system and the character of the social organization. Leach (1947, 239ff.) has examined the difference between Shan and Kachin in terms of the contrast between plough and shifting agriculture. The position in Africa, whether in the savannas or the forest, is somewhat different. But the increase in land a man can bring under cultivation by the use of the plough is apparent in reports from northern Nigeria. Grove noted that in the Dan Yusufu district the average holding of a hoe work-unit was about 8 acres, whereas a mixed farmer using a plough 'requires at least 20 acres of land if he is to make full use of his pair of working cattle' (1957, 40–1). The fact that the amount of good farmland is limited means that only relatively few can adopt this new technique, giving rise to considerable differences in the holding of land. More recently Anthony and Johnston have shown the mean acreage cultivated by plough farmers in this same area was three times as great as that of hoe farmers (1968, 47), though the former also had somewhat larger families.

The increase in productivity that the plough allows has two implications for stratification: it enables a ruling group to develop a much greater standard of living out of the agricultural production (to which, of course, it makes some contribution by way of investment in machinery and protection from interference), but it also means that the producers themselves are ranked on the basis of their command of the means of production, that is, their differential access to land and equipment. Good land for ploughing is now short; not everyone can have as much as he wants. And here we have the basis for the difference between richer and poorer peasants, indeed even landed and landless peasants, that characterises Eurasian village life.

Contrast this kulak situation with the very different rural system described by Burton for one of the most centralized, the most highly organized states in Africa, Dahomey: 'Not a tenth of the land is cultivated; the fallow system is universal, and when a man wants fresh ground he merely brings a little dash to the caboceer' [brings the headman a little 'sweetener'] (1864, 40). Under these conditions, the whole system of stratification, national as well as local, must be very different from the kind of regime where the ruling group has effective control of usufructuary as well as allodial rights. If there is a plentiful supply of land, no man need bend his knee to a lord simply in order to get a living. It is critical to my thesis that in Africa there were no landlord–tenant relationships, nor any institution one can legitimately call 'serfdom' or 'peonage'. Slavery was widespread, though the payoff was limited. Clientship also existed but the rewards for voluntary subjection were either in cattle (as in Ruanda) or in political rights over land, that is, the right to collect tax. It was taxes on trade, gifts from traders, rather than rent or tribute from agricultural activities that contributed to the economy of the ruling class, though income from raiding and from the slaves that this produced was often the most important single source of wealth.

Relations between man and man were rarely based on differences in landholding, either on the state or community level. Indeed, at the community level, land tended to be owned corporately by a lineage group, though exploited by much smaller family units: the lineage might hold fallow land in reserve to be distributed among its members according to need rather than by next-of-kin inheritance (e.g. J. Goody, 1956, 34ff.). While there were differences between rich and poor farmers, these tended to be based upon the strength of one's arm or the number of one's sons, rather than upon the inheritance of landed property. Broadly speaking, poverty was related to labour rather than capital. Indeed many groups conceptualise differences of wealth in terms of strength rather than accumulation. Among the LoDagaa of northern Ghana a poor man is a weak one (*nibaalo*) and a rich man is a strong one (*gandaa, nikpiung*), though the phrase 'chief of money' or 'cowries' (*libie na*) is also used.

Since the social status and living standard of the family groups that exploited the land were little affected by the transmission of the means of production, there was less pressure either to individualise those rights or to channel them to one's offspring. In the centralised states, what counted was the transmission of rights to hold office, where relationship to a particular group (e.g. the ruling Gbanya in Gonja) was often as important as a relationship to a particular person. As far as marriage was concerned, one's daughters were going to get a roughly similar deal (similar to what they had experienced at home) wherever they married, so that selection of mates by property control was less significant. Because of the absence of the plough and other capital investment, land, one man's holding was much like any other. An individual did not have to pursue a policy of marrying people of the same socio-economic class in order to retain differential status, because the differences (other than political ones) were not that great. The relative cultural homogeneity we have observed went hand in hand with the relative economic homogeneity.

Contrast the marriage situation in Europe. To maintain the socio-economic standing of his sons and daughters, a man had to provide them both with part of his property, that is, he had to practice diverging devolution. In the case of a girl, her portion enabled her to acquire a husband who would, in the well-worn phrase, 'maintain her in the standard of life to which she was accustomed'; it also enabled her to support herself in her widowhood through the medium of the dower. It is clear that such a system of property distribution, which involves the establishment of some type of conjugal fund, is difficult to operate unless marriage (marriage with property) is monogamous, and it is highly significant that monogamy is firmly associated with this Eurasian mode of transmitting property.

I have tried to associate certain kinds of marriage arrangements (namely, in-marriage) – which have a fundamental significance for contemporary as well as pre-industrial social structure – with specific ways of passing property between the generations (diverging devolution) and, in turn, to link this with the higher productivity (and scarcer resources) that arise in more advanced systems of agriculture. The contrast is one between Eurasia and Africa, but there is an intermediary area that provides a test of the hypothesis: Ethiopia.

Ethiopia

The nature of the marriage transaction and the relationship to land tenure are
well illustrated in this country, which was African in a geographical but not
in a social sense.

As the main ethnic group, the Amhara, had the plough,[15] land had a considerable economic value. In his account of the area around Dabra Berhan,
Workneh shows how the differences in the standard of living are related to the
ownership of land. While most farmers are poor and 'own only very small
pieces of land', there are 'great differences in the amounts of land possessed.
Some farmers have many pieces of land for farming while others have only
two or three *massa*, an area which may not exceed 30,000 square metres', that
is, about 7.5 acres (1961, 82).

His account further suggests how these differences in landholding are
related to marriage. Sex plays 'a great part in determining the ownership of
land and, in consequence, the standard of living and the type of education
people get... Male children get a greater share of the land than female
children' (1961, 85). In most of Africa a daughter gets no property at all
from her father or whoever controls the surplus of production over consumption; here at least she gets a substantial share, even though, according to the
author, a woman's descendants are poorer than the descendants of sons. At
this point, he seems to disregard a woman's paternal heritage. Her status is
maintained if she marries well, for then her daughter will in turn be properly
provided for by the husband. It is perhaps for this reason that 'parents spend
more money and care on their daughters than on their sons. During childhood
the girls are well dressed while the boys only get enough clothes to protect
themselves from the bitter weather.' The money a parent spends on a girl
clearly affects her ability to attract a husband of the proper socio-economic
standing, although 'even after marriage their parents face many difficulties
and spend much money in supporting their daughters whenever they quarrel
with their husbands'.

Amhara society is differentiated not only in landholding and in standard of
living but also culturally. Rich farmers have different attitudes toward education and religion than the poor, generally being more conservative. But the
village community is only one level of Amharic life. Above it is a massive
secular and religious hierarchy, which is again highly differentiated in terms
of landholding, standard of living, and behaviour. 'The social hierarchy in
traditional Ethiopia', writes Pankhurst, 'was very clearly defined and left its
mark on many facets of everyday life. It could be seen in class relations, in the
use of different forms of speech in addressing or referring to persons of different rank, in different ways of dressing in the presence of superiors, equals

and inferiors, in a series of prohibitions designed to exclude the lower orders from certain privileges in one way or another associated with status, and in the existence of so-called depressed classes' (1961a, 7). These features of the social structure were linked with extreme respect and reticence of the inferior toward the superior and with a large number of sumptuary laws about the wearing of coloured dresses and gold jewellery, the use of umbrellas, as well as more specifically economic privileges like the noble's monopoly on brewing honey wine (*tej*) and the prohibition upon anyone killing a cow 'without leave from the lord of the country' (Alvarez, 1881, 408–9). 'In the time of our fathers and grandfathers', the Tigre nobles declared when giving judgement in a case of this kind, 'persons found with *tej* in their houses were deprived of their land, persons discovered sleeping on leather beds had their riches taken away from them' (Pankhurst, 1961a; see also Pankhurst, 1961b; Levine, 1965).

Differences between statuses and restrictions upon the behaviour of social groups occurred in some centralised states in Africa south of the Sahara, particularly where their economies were based upon military supremacy. My argument is not that such restrictions were absent but that, despite these rules, the African hierarchy, whether of persons or groups, was less highly differentiated in a qualitative sense, even though the number of steps in that hierarchy might be the same as in Eurasia. One reason was the limited amount that upper-status groups were able to remove from the system of agricultural production and the consequent restrictions on the development of economically based subcultures.

Conclusions

In talking of class (in industrial societies) and more generally, of stratification, I do not wish to get involved in the kind of quasi-ideological dispute that has engaged French and American scholars. The point I wish to make is that we need a more subtle vocabulary of hierarchy than the one normally employed. Whatever the differences between Europe and India, Africa certainly differed from both. I speak now of pre-industrial Europe. It is the later Europe, the modern Europe, that Dumont characterises as egalitarian in contrast to the 'hierarchy' of India. In ideological terms he is correct, but the ideology of the French Revolution is at odds with the way the system works, with its implicit stratification, which is more class-like, more caste-like, than the hierarchies of Africa.

The accepted typology of status groups appears to be too abstract and too Eurasian to account for the facts at our command, especially those about Africa where the social groupings in a politically differentiated society are not necessarily in-marrying groups, though many sociologists have seen these as a universal feature of stratified systems. An appreciation of this fact would make for less general and more valid statements. However, I am not simply concerned with social theory in the abstract, nor yet with social history in a more concrete sense, but also with understanding the modern situation (though I would argue that the dichotomy between modern and traditional does not take us very far). The realisation that marriage policy is a variable has important implications for the relationship within and between societies; where integration is desired, exogamy or at least 'preferential out-marriage' (the mixed marriage, in fact) is clearly the most effective way of achieving that end. But here I am primarily concerned with the implications for African societies. There has been a lot of discussion by politicians as well as by sociologists as to the role of classes in the emergent political systems of Africa, much of it dogmatic, ideological, and uninspired. Broadly speaking, African politicians, especially those advocating African socialism, have argued against the existence of a class system in traditional society. For Nkrumah, at least before 1964, Africa was classless; so too for Senghor, Touré, and Nyerere, the last of whom wrote: 'I doubt if the equivalent for the word "class" exists in an indigenous African language; for language describes the ideas of those who speak it, and the idea of "class" and "caste" was non-existent in African society' (1962; 1968, ii). In making such statements, the writers did not mean that there were no status groups in the earlier period, nor that classes (in the European sense) were not now emerging under present conditions. But while European Marxists and non-Marxists alike were attempting to fit Africa into their own developmental schema, these Africans claimed there was an important difference in the socio-economic structure, though they were unable to state clearly what this was. Looking at this whole problem, Grundy has suggested that 'the denial of social classes is a device utilised by ruling elites to bolster their regimes' (1964, 392). As far as the emergent sector goes, this statement undoubtedly holds some truth; our current terminology enables new elites to enjoy high office and high living if their superior position is not stigmatised as 'class'. But there is more to the question than this. As I have tried to show, the traditional system of status groups in African states did differ in major ways from the Eurasian model. African politicians hint at this when they speak of the socialist or communal aspects of land tenure. The Soviet Africanist, I. Potekhin, touched upon the same point when he abandoned his earlier view that Africa displayed a 'patriarchal type of feudalism' and realised that 'in the great majority of African countries the class differentiation of the peasantry is still insignificant' (1963, 39). But much obscurity still remains because the analysis has not been pushed far enough, and neither sociologists nor politicians have tried to answer the crucial question of why such differences existed. When they think about the problem, some writers (e.g. Abraham, 1962) resort to unsatisfactory types of explanations (unsatisfactory because they are circular) which are phrased in terms of the African personality or pan-African culture. Or, like Marx and Weber, they introduce a series of further subdivisions in their types of (for example) feudal or traditional societies, which, if more useful, is still somewhat limiting, since it drowns the attempt to analyse causes or correlatives in a flood of descriptive categorisations.

There is one other concrete aspect of the change connected with the new political, economic, and educational systems in Africa that has received little attention and which is seen particularly clearly when we take up the contrast with Europe. When there is a change in the relative political and economic position of a Eurasian aristocracy, whether because of conquest, democracy, industrialisation, or the rise of new skills, the families involved still have their land and other possessions on which to fall back – providing that the change stops short of complete dispossession. This property gives them a lever on the new dispensation and helps them preserve a privileged position in a changing world. Many European writers have tended to see African chiefships in just such a 'feudal' mode and to ask the same sort of question about the relation between traditional and modern elites as would be appropriate for the post-Reformation period in Europe. As a result, they are anxious to perceive and describe the situation in terms of class conflict. But, except in exceptional cases, African chiefs were sustained by temporary political dominion rather than by persisting economic power (if we can make this crude distinction), and so could put up a little resistance to the changes brought about first by colonial rule and then by independent governments. In any case, chiefs are now a set of individuals, an interest group, rather than a class in the socio-economic sense. Their kin share in their pre-eminence only to a limited extent and easily fit into the modern system, for they have little to gain from sticking to the old. In such a situation, the system of elites (and of stratification generally) is likely to be much more fluid than in Eurasia, and the educational ladder is likely to receive more emphasis as the road to success. 'Africa's golden road', to use Kwesi Armah's less-than-fortunate phrase, lies in the fluidity of its system of stratification, which in turn is related to patterns of marriage and of agricultural production. It is critical to note that in all the post-independence upheaval that has taken place on that continent, little violence has been directed toward superior strata, apart from the colonial rulers themselves. The farmers have risen up against indigenous rulers in two places, Ruanda and Zanzibar, exactly those places where the marriage system stresses the isolation of the political elite. In other parts, the stress upon open *conubium* has tended to produce considerable vertical homogeneity within any area, though this in turn has increased the differentiation between tribes. Thus the greater fluidity of status is counterbalanced by the greater rigidity of tribe; in contemporary Africa the political results of one are as apparent as the other.

The immediate reason lies in the marriage system. Beyond that lies the basic difference in the nature of agricultural production. Under Eurasian conditions, there is a tendency toward close rather than distant marriages, toward in-marriage and endogamy rather than out-marriage and exogamy. Such marriages preserve distinctions of property and status. In Africa, on the other hand, the ownership of land was not the main key to economic achievement. The agricultural output of work-groups varied within fairly confined limits and in this respect the society was relatively homogeneous. Marriage policy was less firmly directed toward the matching of like with like, and more stress could then be placed on the advantages of intermarriage.

Tylor pointed out that exogamy created ties between groups, thus increasing interaction, whereas endogamy was a policy of isolation. When differences in landholding are a major factor in the social hierarchy and when property is conveyed through marriage and inheritance, a premium is placed upon in-marriage rather than out-marriage, upon endogamy rather than exogamy. This is particularly the case where, to preserve the standing of daughters as well as sons, property is distributed bilaterally (that is, to both sexes) by the process of diverging devolution. This policy of isolation leads to variations of behaviour within the culture which tend to crystallise out in gentry sub-cultures or in differences between richer peasants, poorer peasants, and those with no land at all, the rural proletariat.

9. Retrospect

It is pointless to waste time on further conclusions for three reasons. Firstly, at several stages in the book, I have tried briefly to summarise the points I was making. Secondly, such an undertaking has already involved summarising summaries of summaries; scholars of particular societies will want to qualify much of what I have said, and rightly so from an ethnographic standpoint, for the view from the bird's eye does an injustice to the particular richness of life on the ground. But the advance of knowledge involves a perpetual dialectic between general and particular. Thirdly, it would be wrong to tie up too closely what needs to develop more widely: the comparative study of human society, in its full historical, geographical and morphological perspective, has hardly begun to be systematised. The future development of the storage capacity of computers and of the power of analytic programs will increase our ability to handle large quantities of written material for comparative purposes. Despite the inaccuracies of ethnographers, the inefficiency of anthropologists and the woolliness of sociologists, our powers of analysis, our abilities to test our ideas, will be advanced by the increasing sophistication of the technology we create and command.

Not that this is everything. And even without these improved facilities there is plenty of room for the refining and elaboration of general hypotheses. I have tried to sketch out some broad differences in the structure of roles, as category systems and as behavioural systems. But these are only a few of the possible roles that could be examined in this way, and even those that I have mentioned could be looked at from a number of other angles and in a number of other contexts. However the examples I have taken are sufficient to indicate these broad differences, as well as to make the point that in examining the nuclear domestic relationships we need to look at a wider category of roles (e.g. concubine and co-wife, widows and orphans, foster children and foster parents), for people have been too long imprisoned by the idea of the terms for kin as a bounded genealogical set, just as we have failed to pay enough attention to the behaviour, 'ideal' and 'actual', between the individuals who employ them.

The differences I have noted are not tied to the types of economy or society

I have outlined in any absolute way. We are dealing in clusters of interacting variables rather than with biological species. The differences are always statistical, partly because the clusters are not discontinuous, partly because societies are changing, but also because there may be more than one factor behind any particular association we have chosen to examine; for example, in the case of in-marriage, there may be certain circumstances under which this is encouraged in African societies, even though in general peoples tend to marry out.

The central thesis has turned upon the relations between land, 'class', kin and marriage. The link between marriage and social differentiation emerges very clearly in India. Broadly speaking, castes are endogamous groups (i.e. there is an explicit rule of in-marriage); according to Dumont, marriage expresses the separation between groups, which in turn is an expression of 'hierarchy' (1966, 109). Hierarchy integrates the society by reference to its values (252), values which are fundamentally religious; turning Marx on his head, he remarks that the division of labour 'in the last analysis is religious in nature' (153). It is this 'hierarchical principle' which forms a fundamental feature of complex societies other than our own, which are marked by individualism and egalitarianism rather than by holism and hierarchy.

The relation between systems of marriage, of landownership and of 'class' is brought out in Dumont's study, and rather less systematically in some other discussions of the Indian scene. But if we accept the interdependent nature of these features, and of the role relations to which they give rise, we must also recognise that elsewhere states and hierarchies exist which prefer out-marriage, where land is not 'the only recognized wealth', 'closely linked with power over men' (1966, 156). This is the case in most parts of Africa as well as in other areas where we find states based upon extensive agriculture – the African mode of production Coquéry-Vidrovich (1969) has called it, though in referring to other features. Where out-marriage occurs, the strata ('classes') are interlocked by ties of both affinity and kinship, that is, by the presence of 'in-laws', 'mother's brothers' and 'sisters' sons' (or 'fathers' and 'sons' in a matrilineal society) in social groups other than one's own.

The words 'primitive states' have been used of these African kingdoms (Kaberry, 1957) and this term would at least set them aside from the 'hierarchical' states of Asia and the 'feudal' states of pre-modern Europe. But while these states were organisationally simpler than the developing bureaucracies of Eurasia, where the administration had been significantly affected by the use of writing, it is not clear that the epithet 'primitive' provides a very useful description of, say, the Ashanti state in the nineteenth century, as revealed most clearly in the work of Wilks (1975).

Writers on non-European states have attempted a number of different types of categorisation, which all have analytical and theoretical implications. The lumpers have tended to see everything as 'traditional' or 'feudal'; the splitters were lost in particularities; while the middle ground was held by those who distinguished the segmentary states (Southall, 1956), or the snow-ball state (Barnes, 1954). That these studies of state organisation by field workers have been carried out in Africa is not accidental; parallel studies of the more complex states of Asia and Europe have been the preserve of the historian, the political scientist or the sociologist. Some of these have generalised terms like feudal (Coulbourn, 1956); others have adopted concepts such as the Asiatic state or Oriental despotism (Marx and Wittvogel), while some have taken a more Weberian approach in speaking of the historical bureaucratic empires (Eisenstadt, 1963).

Our repertoire of terms is limited, the possibilities infinite, but nevertheless the present context makes it important to differentiate the feudal governments and empires of Europe and Asia from the more complex nation states that developed in Europe after the Renaissance, as well as from the relatively simple (but nevertheless complicated) states that developed in many parts of Africa, which should again be distinguished from the kind of small-scale chief-ship that existed among, say, the Baule of the Ivory Coast or the Ewe of the Togo–Ghana border.

In some respects, these types of state can be seen as representing points on a continuum, differing in degree of centralisation, in number of organisational levels. And yet there are also important differences in kind. The structure of African states was necessarily conditioned by the absence of writing (except where Islam had penetrated) and by the presence of shifting agriculture, in which land is neither a scarce nor a differentiated resource. The literate states (that is, the 'civilisations' of archaeologists, the archaic societies, Asiatic states and Oriental despotisms of Marx and Wittvogel, the 'empires' of Einsenstadt) could develop a more elaborate bureaucracy, a more decisive system of communication, partly because they possessed the art of writing. And at the same time their modes of production were more elaborate because of the mechanisation provided by the plough, the requirements of large-scale irrigation, the development of craft specialisation, combined with the demands of ecclesiastical and political rulers. Equally the nation states of the post-Renaissance period owed much to the development of printing (the mechanisation of writing) for communication, the new firearms that led the way to colonial domination, the improved sea transport that made possible the bulk import of overseas products.

The association between types of state and technological variables is a crude one and the categorisation which emerges from it is certainly not the only useful kind. But it serves a number of purposes and challenges the usual division between Europe and Asia, between class and caste, between equality and hierarchy (Dumont, 1966). From the African standpoint, these other centralised systems are much more similar than they at first appear. For example, each of these main types tends to have its own mode of stratification (I use the word in the most general and neutral sense); modern bureaucracies, with 'classes' in the Weberian sense, constitute stratified systems with an ideology of equality, or anyhow of mobility. The 'empires' tend to have hierarchies in Dumont's sense, consisting of relatively closed status groups, whether of the caste or estate (*ordre*) variety. African states are marked by strata that consist of groups closed for recruitment but open to marriage, ones which are not differentiated, as in the empires, with regard to the basic means of agricultural production, though they may be with regard to the ownership of those who can exploit these open resources (namely, slaves), with regard to the control of trade, or with regard to the ownership of the means of destruction (J. Goody, 1971b). This fact means that both on the societal, local and individual scale, stratification take on a different character; above all, frequent intermarriage implies a limit to the development of internal cultural differences.

In arguing about the interrelationships between social groups in a hierarchy, and the difference made by frequent marriage between strata, I did not intend to be making an absolute distinction between class conflict with endogamy and cooperation without. I am not attempting to put forward a 'functional' theory of the integration of orders such as appears to lie behind some of the writings of Mousnier (1969) on feudal Europe and of numerous others on African and Asian topics. But there do seem important differences in the relationship between groups and individuals in the social hierarchy which have to be phrased in economic as well as ideological terms. In so doing, one can try and specify, in more or less precise ways, how the system of domestic relations, of family, kin and marriage, organises (and is organised by) the productive and reproductive processes, ensuring the continuity but not perpetuity of a particular socio-economic system.

In seeing systems of kinship as being related to the economic and political differences between states in Africa and Eurasia, I am not of course denying the existence of other important differences that cannot be explained in this way. Nor am I trying to assign a universal preeminence to (or determination by) economic or material factors, though their role, 'in the last instance', I take as given (a statement I find neither very surprising nor very illuminating).

Let me touch upon the second of these points. One does not have to be a 'vulgar materialist' to understand that hunters and gatherers do not have centralised systems of government. Except at this level, there is unlikely to be a one-to-one relationship between economy and polity; similar agricultural economies were to be found in Africa in both states and non-state areas (i.e.

acephalous 'tribes'), so that while agriculture is a necessary condition for states, it is not a sufficient condition and we need to search for the other relevant factors, which may certainly include religious and ideological ones. In some circumstances the latter may not merely be contributory but 'dominant'. For example, certain written codes which I find to be consistent with, even expressions of, diverging devolution, may be extended to other very different types of society by the process of imperial conquest or religious conversion. It is in precisely this way that Christian (European), Muslim and Buddhist codes have reached out into areas that might otherwise have retained features we have associated with the separation of male and female property. For example, Islam encourages marriage to the father's brother's daughter, a union that breaks down the exogamous nature of the patriclan and is often associated with the retention of some relatively exclusive characteristic (e.g. property) within the paternal family. In some cases the causal chain or arc takes one direction; in other cases a different one. And we have always to allow for movement in the reverse direction, for feedback, for ebb as well as flow. For example, if I have treated kinship terms as the dependent variable in certain path diagrams, I by no means exclude the possibility that the use of specific terms influences the marriage choices of individuals, though I regard this influence as going against the dominant current.

Most of our models, framed in terms of idealist or materialist assumptions, of the dominance of superstructure or infrastructure, of the preeminence of words or things, are too simple, too crude, too linear, too flat-footed, to deal with these subtleties, except by reversion to the unhelpful models of a functionalist or structuralist, of the Gestalt or systems-theory kind, unhelpful because it is of little advantage to know that everything is related to everything else, on any of the possible levels, unless it it also possible to show the extent to which it is so related, to demonstrate the non-fit as well as the fit. We need to be able to make some assessment of partial fits, of relative homogeneities, of degrees of inter-relatedness, and at present such developments are only possible through the use of some kind of numerical technique, which goes a stage beyond verbal or graphic formalisation.

This I tried to do by examining the relation between a mode of inheritance (or more broadly of devolution) which preserved the relative status of both sons and daughters, that is, diverging devolution, and various other aspects of social life. The necessity of preserving such status appeared to be linked to advanced agriculture, an economy that produced a significant surplus and a hierarchical social order where each group tried to maintain or improve its position. The implication on the domestic level was inmarriage or up-marriage, i.e. homogamy or hypergamy. The implication for inheritance was the concentration upon close kin, indeed upon one's own direct descendants, the shift from lateral to lineal, from sideways to downwards. There were implications, too, for the control of the sexuality of girls, since they were in many cases holders, or anyhow carriers, of property, sometimes landed property. Hence we would expect to find an emphasis on the prohibition of pre-marital sex, and upon the role of the chaperone, the go-between and the marriage broker in arranging 'proper' matches. Moreover marriage, once made, was likely to be difficult to repeat (i.e. to be monogamous) and difficult to break (i.e. to have low rates of divorce).

The implications for the structure of roles were examined in a more impressionistic way. I argued that under dowry systems, marriage transactions tend to be differentiated both between and within strata. It is often in the upper groups that the father provides for his daughter, and in the lower where an indirect dowry, supplied by the groom or his kin, plays a more important part. But in any case, where marriage is linked with property transactions (or with future transactions) in this way, then the status of the sexual partner tends to be differentiated in category terms depending upon whether she was married with dowry (as a wife) or without (as a concubine); in this, the situation seemed strikingly different from the jurally equal situation between co-wives in Africa, where property entered into marriage transactions in a very different way, by bridewealth rather than by dowry.

The distribution of other roles was also seen to be linked to this same central difference; moreover, the quality of the interaction differs in significant ways, as, for example, in the case of step-parents and step-children, since these relationships were often influenced by the anticipation or actuality of inheritance. So too were a number of other close relationships, that between uncles and nephews, and possibly between brothers and sisters.

Not only should we expect the relationships to differ, but also the strategies of individuals in terms of their 'life-chances'. The distribution of adoption seems to be closely linked with societies where the direct continuity of property and descent receives much emphasis, as a means of maintaining and continuing status. Adoption is simply one of a set of possible strategies of heirship and of continuity, which are dependent not only upon specifically 'demographic' parameters, but also upon a range of social factors that influence those parameters and affect the way in which the system of social differentiation and control is reproduced. The reproduction of such differences underpins the social hierarchy itself, and in the final chapter an attempt is made to relate aspects of marriage and property to the system of stratification and to the means of production. It is here that we see the central differences of production and reproduction in Africa on the one hand and Europe and Asia on the other, differences that have to be interpreted not only in specific cultural terms but also in the wider context of the broad historical changes in man's social life.

Appendix I. Tables

(For Table 1 see p. 12)

TABLE 2 *Prohibited premarital sexual behaviour and diverging devolution*

	Prohibition on premarital sex		
	Present	Absent	Total
Diverging devolution:			
Present	56	32	88
Absent	74	110	184
No individual property rights or no rule of transmission	29	20	49

1. Top quadrant:	Total of table	321
phi = 0.21	N.I. on devolution	271
$\chi^2 = 12.16$	N.I. on sexual relations	248
$p < 0.001$	Sexual relations precluded by very early marriage age	23
		863
2. 'No rights', etc. added to 'absent':		
phi = 0.17		
$\chi^2 = 8.89$		
$p < 0.01$		

N.B. The prohibition is coded in col. 78: P, V = present, A, F, T = absent.

TABLE 3 *Endogamy and diverging devolution*

	Endogamy		
	Present	Absent	Total
Diverging devolution:			
Present	37	121	158
Absent	34	318	352
No individual property rights or no rule of transmission	4	73	77

1. Top quadrant: phi = 0.18 $\chi^2 = 16.09$ $p < 0.001$	Total of table 587 N.I. on devolution 271 N.I. on endogamy 5
2. 'No rights', etc. added to 'absent': phi = 0.19 $\chi^2 = 20.68$ $p < 0.001$	863

N.B. Endogamy is coded in col. 19: D = present: E, C, T, S, A = absent; and in col. 69: C, E = present: D, O = absent.

TABLE 4 *Father's brother's daughter marriage and diverging devolution*

	Father's brother's daughter marriage			
	Preferred	Permitted	Prohibited	Total
Diverging devolution:				
Present	13	26	108	147
Absent	5	14	295	314
No individual property rights or no rule of transmission	0	1	72	73

1. Top quadrant (permitted and preferred together) phi = 0.28 $\chi^2 = 36.34$ $p < 0.001$	Total of table 534 N.I. on devolution 271 N.I. on FBD marriage 58 863
2. 'No rights', etc. added to 'absent' (permitted and preferred together): phi = 0.30 $\chi^2 = 47.32$ $p < 0.001$	

N.B. Col 25 codes cross-cousin marriage: D, F, Q = Father's brother's daughter marriage permitted; col 26, a = preferred, col. 25, no entry = N.I.; the remainder are negative.

TABLE 5   *Monogamy and diverging devolution*

	Monogamy		
	Present	Absent	Total
Diverging devolution:			
Present	58	101	159
Absent	30	325	355
No individual property rights or no rule of transmission	10	66	76

1. Top quadrant:	Total of table	590
phi = 0.34	N.I. on devolution	271
$\chi^2 = 58.83$	N.I. on monogamy	2
$p < 0.001$		863
2. 'No rights', etc. added to 'absent':		
phi = 0.32		
$\chi^2 = 60.08$		
$p < 0.001$		

N.B. Monogamy is coded in col. 14 or 15, M = present; col. 14 or 15, other entries = absent.

TABLE 6   *Residence and diverging devolution*

	Alternative residence		
	Present	Absent	Total
Diverging devolution:			
Present	57	103	160
Absent	53	302	355
No individual property rights or no rule of transmission	34	43	77

1. Top quadrant:	Total of table	592
phi = 0.23	N.I. on devolution	271
$\chi^2 = 26.90$		
$p < 0.001$		863
2. 'No rights', etc. added to 'absent':		
phi = 0.16		
$\chi^2 = 14.38$		
$p < 0.001$		

N.B. Alternative residence here includes neolocal residence (see text): it is coded in cols. 17 and 18: Pu, Pm, Vu, Vm, N (including all alternatives in col. 18) = present. Others = absent.

TABLE 7   *Residence, bilateral kinship and diverging devolution*

			Residence		
	Bilocal	Neolocal	Virilocal with uxorilocal alternatives (Pu, Vu, Pm, Vm)	Other	Total
Diverging devolution:					
Present	19	23	15	103	160
Absent	8	10	35	301	354
No individual property rights or no rule of transmission	17	0	17	43	77
Bilateral kinship:					
Present	52	31	73	152	308
Absent	11	13	38	487	549

TABLE 8   *Diverging devolution and sibling kin terms*

	Sibling kin terms		
	Present	Absent	Total
Diverging devolution:			
Present	60	85	145
Absent	43	228	271
No individual property rights or no rule of transmission	6	67	73

1. Top quadrant:
   phi $= 0.28$ Total of table   489
   $\chi^2 = 31.65$ N.I. on devolution   271
   $p < 0.001$ N.I. on kin terms   103
2. 'No rights', etc. added to 'absent':   863
   phi $= 0.29$
   $\chi^2 = 41.81$
   $p < 0.001$

N.B. Figures are derived from col. 27, D, E = present. Others = absent.
Present includes the Eskimo and descriptive categories. As defined in the code, Sudanese and Iroquois terminologies may also include cases where siblings are differentiated from all other cousins. In Table 7 these terminologies have been included in the negative cases but another test could be run showing Iroquois and Sudanese as a mixed category.

TABLE 9   *Diverging devolution and plough agriculture*

	Plough agriculture		
	Present	Absent	Total
Diverging devolution:			
Present	60	100	160
Absent	47	308	355
No individual property rights or no rule of transmission	0	77	77

1. Top quadrant:	Total of table	592
phi = 0.27	N.I. on devolution	271
$\chi^2 = 37.98$		
$p < 0.001$		
2. 'No rights', etc. added to 'absent':		863
phi = 0.30		
$\chi^2 = 54.09$		
$p < 0.001$		

N.B. Plough is coded in col. 39: present = 2, 3; absent = 1. The absence of an entry might mean no plough or no information.

TABLE 10   *Diverging devolution and intensive agriculture*

	Intensive agriculture		
	Present	Absent	Total
Diverging devolution:			
Present	87	73	160
Absent	108	247	355
No individual property rights or no rule of transmission	3	74	77

1. Top quadrant:	Total of table	592
phi = 0.22	N.I. on devolution	271
$\chi^2 = 25.89$		
$p < 0.001$		863
2. 'No rights', etc. added to 'absent':		
phi = 0.27		
$\chi^2 = 41.87$		
$p < 0.001$		

N.B. Intensive agriculture is coded in col. 28: present = I, J; absent = others.

TABLE 11   *Diverging devolution and stratification (caste and class)*

	Stratification		
	Present	Absent	Total
Diverging devolution:			
Present	49	110	159
Absent	28	321	349
No individual property rights or no rule of transmission	1	76	77

1. Top quadrant:
   phi = 0.29
   x^2 = 42.38
   p < 0.001
2. 'No rights', etc. added to 'absent':
   phi = 0.31
   x^2 = 55.70
   p < 0.001

Total of table	585
N.I. on devolution	271
N.I. on stratification	7
	863

N.B. Caste here is the category coded C in col. 69; class is C and E in col. 67.

TABLE 12   *Diverging devolution and large states*

	Large states		
	Present	Absent	Total
Diverging devolution:			
Present	41	112	153
Absent	33	315	348
No individual property rights or no rule of transmission	0	77	77

1. Top quadrant:
   phi = 0.22
   x^2 = 23.95
   p < 0.001
2. 'No rights', etc. added to 'absent':
   phi = 0.25
   x^2 = 34.82
   p < 0.001

Total of table	578
N.I. on devolution	271
N.I. on polity	14
	863

N.B. Large states is coded in col. 33: 3, 4 = present; 0, 1, 2 = absent.

TABLE 13 *Diverging devolution and in-marriage*

	In-marriage		
	Present	Absent	Total
Diverging devolution:			
Present	67	93	160
Absent	46	307	353
No individual property rights or no rule of transmission	4	73	77

1. Top quadrant:	Total of table	590
phi = 0.32	N.I. on devolution	271
$\chi^2 = 51.66$	N.I. on in-marriage	2
$p < 0.001$		863

2. 'No rights', etc. added to 'absent':
    phi = 0.32
    $\chi^2 = 65.22$
    $p < 0.001$

N.B. In-marriage is coded in col. 19: no entry or s = no information; D = present; col. 25: no entry = no information; Q, D, or F = present; col. 26: A = present; and col. 69: no entry = no information; E, C = present. Other entries = absent.

TABLE 14 *Diverging devolution and advanced agriculture*

	Advanced agriculture		
	Present	Absent	Total
Diverging devolution:			
Present	90	70	160
Absent	117	238	355
No individual property rights or no rule of transmission	3	74	77

1. Top quadrant:	Total of table	592
phi = 0.22	N.I. on devolution	271
$\chi^2 = 23.93$		863
$p < 0.001$		

2. 'No rights', etc. added to 'absent':
    phi = 0.26
    $\chi^2 = 40.12$
    $p < 0.001$

N.B. Advanced agriculture is coded in col. 28: no entry = no information; I, J = present; O, C, E, H = absent; col. 39: q, p = present; no entry = absent or no information.

TABLE 15   *Diverging devolution and complex polity.*

	Complex polity		
	Present	Absent	Total
Diverging devolution:			
Present	57	102	159
Absent	47	308	355
No individual property rights or no rule	1	76	77
of transmission			

1. Top quadrant: Total on table   591
  phi = 0.25   N.I. on devolution   271
  $\chi^2 = 33.40$ N.I. on complex polity   1
  $p < 0.001$ —
2. 'No rights', etc. added to 'absent':   863
  phi = 0.28
  $\chi^2 = 47.00$
  $p < 0.001$

N.B. Complex polity is coded in col. 33: no entry = no information; 3, 4 = present; col. 67: no entry = no information; c = present. Other entries = absent.

TABLE 16   *Sex roles in agriculture and advanced agriculture*

		Advanced agriculture		
		Present	Absent	Total
Female farming		42	191	233
Male farming		121	83	204
	Total	163	274	437

phi = 0.42   Total of table   437
$\chi^2 = 77.53$ Equal participation   205
$p < 0.001$ No agriculture   188
            N.I. on agriculture   33
              Total   863

N.B. Sex roles in agriculture are coded from col. 62: F, G = female farming; M, N = male farming; D, E = equal participation; O = no agriculture; no entry = no information.
Advanced agriculture is coded from cols. 28 and 39. Col. 28:I, J = present; C, E, H, O = absent; no entry = no information. col. 39: q, p = present; no entry = absent or no information.

TABLE 17   *Sex roles in agriculture and community size*

Size	Female farming		Male farming		Equal participation		Total
0–99	35⎫	(77.8%)	17⎫	(40.9%)	33⎫	(63.3%)	85
100–399	56⎭		32⎭		36⎭		124
400–1,000	19⎫	(22.2%)	16⎫	(59.1%)	15⎫	(36.7%)	50
1,000 +	7⎭		55⎭		25⎭		87
Total	117		120		109		346

Taking the figures for male and female   Total of table   346
  farming as against large and small size of No agriculture   188
  local community: N.I. on agriculture   33
  $\chi^2 = 33.44$ (df $= 1$)   N.I. on community size   296
  $p < 0.001$ Total   863

N.B. Sex roles in agriculture are coded as in Table 16. Community size is coded in col. 31: $1 + 2 = 0$–99; $3 + 4 = 100$–399; $5 = 400$–1,000; $6 + 7 + 8 = 1,000+$; 0 or no entry $=$ no information. (Communities where agriculture is absent are mainly of small size.)

TABLE 18   *Sex roles in agriculture and plurality of marriage*

	No agriculture	Female farming	Male farming	Equal partici-pation	Total
Monogamy	16 (8.6%)	19 (8.2%)	57 (28.4%)	38 (18.5%)	130
Limited polygyny	98 (52.7%)	65 (28.0%)	82 (40.8%)	82 (40.0%)	327
General polygyny	72 (38.7%)	148 (63.8%)	62 (30.8%)	85 (41.5%)	367
Total	186	232	201	205	824

$\chi^2 = 81.27$ (df $= 6$)   Total of table   824
$p < 0.001$ N.I. on agriculture   33
                                         N.I. on plurality of marriage   6

                                                Total   863

N.B. Sex roles in agriculture are coded in col. 62: O $=$ no agriculture; F, G $=$ female farming; M, N $=$ male farming; D, E $=$ equal participation; no entry, I, P $=$ no information. Plurality of marriage is coded in cols. 14 and 15: M $=$ monogamy; N $=$ limited polygyny, G, F, E in col. 14, R, S, Q, P in either col. $=$ general polygyny; O, no entry in col. 14 and in col. 15 $=$ no information.

TABLE 19   *Sex roles in agriculture and marriage transactions*

	No agriculture	Female farming	Male farming	Equal participation	Total
Bridewealth	51 (27.1%)	135 (58.4%)	85 (41.7%)	116 (56.6%)	387
Bride service	30 (16.0%)	27 (11.7%)	16 (7.8%)	19 (9.3%)	92
Gift exchange and sister exchange	33 (17.6%)	20 (8.7%)	10 (4.9%)	15 (7.3%)	78
Dowry	2 (1.1%)	0 (0.0%)	15 (7.4%)	7 (3.4%)	24
No payment taken	72 (38.3%)	49 (21.2%)	78 (38.2%)	48 (23.4%)	247
Total	188	231	204	205	828

$\chi^2 = 93.93$ (df $= 12$)
$p < 0.001$

Total of table	828
N.I. on agriculture	33
N.I. on marriage transactions	2
Total	863

N.B. Sex roles in agriculture are coded in col. 62: O = no agriculture; F, G = female farming; D, E = equal participation; M, N = male farming; no entry, I, P = no information; Marriage transactions are coded in col. 12: B = brideprice; S = brideservice; G, X = gift/sister exchange; D = dowry; T, O = no payment taken; no entry = no information.

(For Table 20 see p. 34)

TABLE 21 *Sex participation in agriculture by continent*

Sex participation	Africa	Circum-Mediterranean	East Eurasia	Insular Pacific	North America	South America	Total
Female farming	125 (53.9%)	4 (4.7%)	7 (7.6%)	36 (29.8%)	29 (13.6%)	32 (37.6%)	233
Male farming	39 (16.8%)	56 (65.1%)	32 (34.8%)	28 (23.1%)	28 (13.1%)	21 (24.7%)	204
Equal participation	60 (25.9%)	22 (25.6%)	41 (44.6%)	48 (39.7%)	12 (5.6%)	22 (25.9%)	205
No agriculture	8 (3.4%)	4 (4.7%)	12 (13.0%)	9 (7.4%)	145 (67.8%)	10 (11.8%)	188
Total	232	86	92	121	214	85	830

Total of table 830
N.I. on agriculture 33
Total 863

$\chi^2 = 504.55$ (df = 15)
$p < 0.001$

N.B. Sex participation in agriculture is coded from col. 62: F, G = female farming; M, N = male farming; D, E = equal participation; O = no agriculture; no entry = no information.

TABLE 22 *Revised matrix of devolution variables for linkage and path analysis*

	Diverging devolution	Male farming	Prohibited premarital sex	Sibling kin terms	Advanced agriculture	Complex polity	In-marriage	Monogamy
Diverging devolution		0.40	0.21	0.28	0.22	0.25	0.32	0.34
Male farming	0.40		0.19	0.29	0.42	0.26	0.33	0.26
Prohibited sex premarital	0.21	0.19		0.14	0.13	0.23	0.08	0.00
Sibling kin terms	0.28	0.29	0.14		0.32	0.28	0.26	0.23
Advanced agriculture	0.22	0.42	0.13	0.32		0.41	0.22	0.20
Complex polity	0.25	0.26	0.23	0.28	0.41		0.30	0.18
In-marriage	0.32	0.33	0.08	0.26	0.22	0.30		0.15
Monogamy	0.34	0.26	0.00	0.23	0.20	0.18	0.15	

(For Tables 23, 24 and 25 see pages 57, 74 and 88)

Appendix 2. The probability of family distributions

(With G. A. Harrison)

The following table illustrates the variations in the composition of families depending on the average size and the likelihood of a child dying before his father. For present purposes we assume that a 'modern' population is represented in the top left-hand corner, and a pre-industrial one in the bottom right. The figure of one-third chance of a son succeeding his father corresponds roughly to pre-industrial conditions, the figure of two-thirds corresponds roughly to the contemporary situation. The families consist of couples who can have children; this figure represents approximately 95 per cent of married couples since about 5 per cent (the sterility figure is variable) are unable to have children and can therefore be added to the number of families with no heirs.

Assuming that populations were only increasing slowly before the advent of modern medicine, the average proportions of families with no heirs, with daughters only and with male heirs, would remain roughly the same over time. E. A. Wrigley estimates the proportion as 20:20:60. On the table below this figure would correspond to a family size of 6 with a one-third chance of a son surviving a father (i.e. two-thirds chance of dying before his father), where the figures (before the 5 per cent adjustment) would read 12 (no heirs), 23 (daughters), 65 (male heir); corrected the figure would read 17:21:62.[1]

In Table 25 below we have assumed a sex ratio of 100.

(i) Any population to which this table is applied should be homogeneous. The effect of populations made up of two or more distinct groups with their own parameters is discussed below.

(ii) Death after a live birth is assumed to be random; hence no account is taken of the fact that diseases may strike several members of the same household and miss other households completely, to a greater extent than this assumption of randomness would allow for.

While the distribution may remain relatively constant under pre-industrial conditions, the growth in population would produce significant changes. When average family size drops as mortality decreases with improved medical conditions, the proportion of heirless families rises.

Even in the situation of low population growth, the understanding of the demographic variations underlying strategies of heirship is of some use. Different strata within a 'stable' population may have differing average sizes of families; for example, larger household sizes among higher status groups have been widely reported for India (Lewis, 1958, 18), China (Freedman, 1970, 3), and Japan (T. C. Smith, 1959, 7), groups in which mortality is presumably lower.[2] These differences within a population, which will be reflected in differences in the number of possible female heirs and fraternal households, may contain an element that ensures upward and downward mobility. For Yunan, Fei and Chang have shown how, among richer peasants, larger families led to greater subdivision and hence a change in status relative to the critical factor of land-holding (1948, 117). The position of kulaks (as distinct from the large landholders, the gentry) was an impermanent one. Thus within a relatively 'stable' population, there may be much internal differentiation and many internal changes that relate to the distribution of heirs and the associated strategies.

133

TABLE 26   *Probability of family distributions (as percentages)*

Probability of child dying before father		Average family size (number of children)							
		2.5	3.0	3.5	4.0	4.5	5.0	5.5	6.0
0.3	A	24.3	22.7	20.7	18.6	16.4	14.4	12.5	10.7
	B	17.4	12.2	8.6	6.1	4.3	3.0	2.1	1.5
	C	36.5	36.7	36.0	34.5	32.6	30.4	28.1	25.7
	D	21.9	28.3	34.6	40.9	46.7	52.2	57.3	62.1
	A	24.7	23.5	21.8	19.8	17.8	15.8	13.9	12.2
	B	19.7	14.2	10.3	7.4	5.4	3.9	2.8	2.0
	C	36.1	36.8	36.5	35.4	33.9	32.0	29.9	27.7
	D	19.5	25.5	31.4	37.3	43.0	48.3	53.3	58.0
0.4	A	24.9	24.1	22.7	21.0	19.2	17.3	15.5	13.8
	B	22.3	16.5	12.2	9.1	6.7	5.0	3.7	2.7
	C	35.4	36.0	36.7	36.1	35.0	33.5	31.7	29.8
	D	17.4	22.8	28.3	33.8	39.1	44.2	49.1	53.7
0.45	A	25.0	24.6	23.6	22.2	20.6	18.9	17.2	15.5
	B	25.3	19.2	14.6	11.1	8.4	6.4	4.9	3.7
	C	34.6	36.2	36.8	36.6	35.9	34.8	33.3	31.7
	D	15.2	20.0	25.1	30.1	35.1	39.9	44.6	49.1
0.5	A	24.9	24.9	24.3	23.3	21.9	20.4	18.9	17.3
	B	28.7	22.3	17.4	13.5	10.5	8.2	6.4	5.0
	C	33.5	35.4	36.5	36.8	36.5	35.8	34.8	33.5
	D	13.1	17.4	21.9	26.4	31.0	35.6	39.9	44.2
0.55	A	24.5	25.0	24.8	24.1	23.1	21.9	20.6	19.2
	B	32.5	25.9	20.7	16.5	13.2	10.5	8.4	6.7
	C	32.1	34.4	35.8	36.6	36.8	36.5	35.9	35.0
	D	11.0	14.7	18.7	22.8	26.9	31.0	35.1	39.1
0.6	A	23.9	24.8	25.0	24.7	24.1	23.3	22.2	21.0
	B	36.8	30.1	24.7	20.2	16.5	13.5	11.1	9.1
	C	30.3	32.9	34.8	35.9	36.6	36.8	36.6	36.1
	D	9.0	12.2	15.6	19.1	22.8	26.4	30.1	33.8
0.65	A	22.9	24.2	24.8	25.0	24.8	24.3	23.6	22.7
	B	41.7	35.0	29.4	24.7	20.7	17.4	14.6	12.2
	C	28.2	31.1	33.2	34.8	35.8	36.5	36.8	36.7
	D	7.2	9.8	12.6	15.6	18.7	21.9	25.1	28.3

Key: A—only daughters   B—no heirs   C—one son   D—two or more sons.

Notes

1. The evolution of the domestic economy

1 For a thorough and judicious comment upon McLennan's work, see P. Rivière's introduction to the new edition of *Primitive Marriage*, Chicago, 1970.

2 J. S. Black and G. W. Chrystal, *William Robertson Smith*, London, 1912.

3 Vol. 13, 253–79.

4 See A. R. Radcliffe-Brown (1950), but the point had earlier been made by C. N. Starcke (1894) and C. S. Wake (1967): see Rivière 1970, xxxviii.

5 By 'descent' and 'alliance' theorists, I refer to those who stress kinship and marriage respectively, or again reproduction and 'exchange'. A more precise use is to define descent in terms of membership of unilineal kin groups, e.g. clans or lineages, and alliance in terms of continuing affinal arrangements between groups (or sometimes categories), e.g. cross-cousin marriage. By 'extensionists' I refer to those who see wider kinship ties as extensions of the family outwards; by 'categorists', those who interpret these relationships in terms of the social structure as a whole, and who therefore place as much emphasis on the categorical aspects of kin terms as upon their particular, individual reference.

6 Talcott Parsons, *Societies in Evolutionary and Comparative Perspectives*, Englewood Cliffs, N.J., 1966.

7 And earlier by Murdock (1937a; 1959).

8 For a discussion of some of the issues involved, see T. D. Graves, N. B. Graves and M. J. Korbin, 'Historical Inferences from Guttman Scales: the return of the age-area magic', *Current Anthropology*, 10 (1969), 317–38.

9 I refer specifically to Eskimo, Hawaiian and Descriptive terminologies for cousins as defined by G. P. Murdock, Ethnographic Atlas: a summary *Ethnography*, 6 (1967), 109–236: see my discussion in J. Goody, 1970b.

10 See D. B. Heath, Sexual Division of Labor and Cross-Cultural Research, *Soc. Forces*, 37 (1958), 77–9; M. F. Nimkoff and R. Middleton, Types of Family and Types of Economy, *Am. J. Sociol.*, 46 (1960), 215–25.

11 G. P. Murdock, *Social Structure in Southeast-Asia*, Chicago, 1960.

12 This kind of question has been more vigorously pursued by others. On polygyny, see R. Clignet, *Many Wives, Many Powers*, Northwestern University Press, 1970. On agricultural development and social organization, see Ester Boserup, *Women's Role in Economic Development*, George Allen & Unwin, 1970.

13 Bosman was accustomed to the conjugal community of Roman Dutch Law. But the absence of a dowry was apparent even to Englishmen reared under the qualified unity of conjugal property which was a feature of their Common Law. This broad distinction between Africa and Europe still persists. 'Marriage in Ashanti between free persons . . . does not lead to community of property between the spouses, still less to the sinking of the wife's legal persona in her husband's' (Allott, 1966, 191).

14 The absence of a dowry is enshrined in local usage of English and French. For the

135

Europeans, having no word for prestations that passed from the family of the groom to that of the bride, used the word they had, 'dot' or 'dowry', for a very different set of transactions. These terms are still sometimes used for 'bridewealth' and other prestations.

15 Barton used the term 'homoparental' but this presents difficulties for matrilineal inheritance.

16 Noted for example by Goode, 1963, 167.

17 P. Vinogradoff, *Outlines of Historical Jurisprudence*, vol. 1: Introduction – *Tribal Law*, London 1920, p. 292; J. R. Goody, *Death, Property and the Ancestors*, Stanford, Calif., 1962, 311.

18 I initially raised this point in 'The mother's brother and the sister's son in West Africa', *J. R. Anthrop. Inst.*, 89 (1959), 51–88, reprinted in *Comparative Studies in Kinship*, London, 1969.

19 The same, 81. See also *Death, Property and the Ancestors*, 315.

20 Germaine Tillion (1966) refers to indirect dowry as *douaire* (dower).

21 As among the Ijaw of Nigeria, the Nyamwezi of Tanzania and the eastern Bamileke of Cameroons.

2. The theory, the variables and a test

1 J. Goody 1962, v.

2 I have used all the data from the *Atlas* and have not sampled it in the way suggested by Murdock, 1967, 114. The reasons for this are purely practical. I have conducted further tests on samples which bear out the general conclusions (Buckley and Goody, 1974).

3 The phi coefficient is also known as the Kendall partial rank coefficient (Siegel, 1956, 225–6).

4 I also speak of the 'woman's property complex', referring to her access to property held by males. Under systems of homogeneous inheritance, women have property but it is either inherited from women or self-acquired.

5 This entry has been shown separately on the tables as it could be argued (in some cases) that it is equivalent to the absence of diverging devolution.

6 Property was also destroyed during the lifetime of the holder in the well-known case of the potlatch.

7 See Jane Austen's *Northanger Abbey* for an example of the role of the chaperone.

8 See Goody, 'Incorporation and marriage policy in Northern Ghana' (1969d).

9 For definitions of these terms, see Murdock, 1967, 166.

10 The kind of property is also relevant; it may be more important to keep intact a farm or an estate than a hoard of gold coins or safe full of share certificates.

11 If monogamy and polyandry are included together as positive cases, the association with diverging devolution gives a phi of 0.37 ($p < 0.001$).

12 Logically, neolocal residence is less firmly attached to diverging devolution than are bilocal or the less evenly distributed systems of alternative residence. But the boundaries of 'neolocal' residence are difficult to discriminate (how separate is 'separate'?).

13 In my account of the LoWiili of Northern Ghana (1956), I suggested that the increased differentiation of wealth militated against the movement of property outside the co-residential group. The specific feature of this group that inhibits a dispersal of the property is its character as a unit of production. Where self-acquired property ('income') begins to play a greater part than inherited wealth ('capital'), then there will be increasing reluctance to allow property to go outside, as is bound to be the case where the residential pattern is incongruent (or partially so, as in a fully fledged system of double descent) with the mode of inheritance.

14 This point is developed in Chapter 6.
15 Alliance theory is associated not only with complex societies practising diverging devolution, but also with simple societies where inheritance plays little part, e.g. Australia. The bimodal distribution of certain forms of cousin marriage, or more generally of marriage exchange, may be partly responsible for leaving obscured the underlying relationship to rights over property and, more generally, to productive systems.

3. Making causal inferences

1 See Henry Grey Graham on the effects of increasing wealth in mid eighteenth century Scotland on forcing apart the status groups (1899 [1937], 261ff.)
2 According to Grove (1961, 123), 2 acres is 'rather a large acreage per head for African hand farmers to cultivate', allowing a population density of 160 per square mile. The acreage a plough could cultivate depended of course upon the type of land and its mode of tenure. According to Graham (1899 [1937], 156), the heavy wooden Scottish plough used before the agricultural changes of the mid eighteenth century could scratch only half an acre a day, 'and scratched it very poorly'.

4. Farming, labour and sex

1 If we simply test the association of male and female farming against monogamy and polygyny without taking any account of the rates of polygyny, the phi result is 0.26.
2 The previous analyses were based upon the McQuitty procedure, which averages the correlation coefficients. The present technique, for which we are indebted to J. C. Mitchell of Nuffield College, Oxford, avoids this problem.
3 He continues, 'I have arbitrarily omitted all paths of less than 1. The difficulties at the moment are the relatively strong path between Complex polity and Prohibited premarital sex, and the lack of the path between Prohibited premarital sex and Sibling kin terms.' (Personal communication.) It should be added that Barrie Irving has also tested the data by means of the A.I.D. (Automatic Interaction Detector) which is a step-wise multiple regression analysis that attempts to find the best set of predictors by automatic methods, described by Sonquist, Baker and Morgan in Searching for Structure (1973). By this technique, we tried to compare the division of labour by sex (i.e. 'male farming') and diverging devolution. The preliminary results suggest that devolution is a better predictor than the division of labour by sex.
4 For a review of the earlier discussions, see Lowie 1937.

5. Concubines and co-wives

1 In fact for Radcliffe-Brown the elements of a social structure are persons, while roles are elements of an organisation (1952, 10–11).
2 See Dorjahn, 1959, 102; this figure is the mean percentage of all married men who are polygynous in sub-Saharan Africa.
3 Boserup, 1970, 48, quoting Appodorai, 1954, 18. For the Moroccan figures, see Adam 1968, 734.
4 See Chapter 6 below and my article on 'Polygyny, economy and the role of women', in J. Goody (ed.), Character of Kinship, Cambridge, 1973. Of course, in Eurasia there is also an element of conspicuous consumption in polygyny, as in other forms of expenditure, and in the Islamic world today the incidence of plural marriages tends to be higher among the traditional bourgeoisie.

5   The idea that one only 'blesses' a union once it had been shown to be durable exists today in the West Indies.

6   Bracton, *De Legibus*, lib. iii, tract. ii. c. 28., para 1, and lib. iv, tract. vi. c. 8, para. 4.

7   In Babylon, one form of secondary union appears to have been accompanied by property.

8   The situation has changed under the Marriage Law of 1950 which prohibited concubinage and child betrothal, and encouraged widow remarriage.

9   See 'Polygyny, economy and the role of women' in J. Goody (ed.), *Character of Kinship*, Cambridge, 1973.

10   Juvenal, *The Sixteen Satires*, translated by Peter Green, Penguin Books, 1967.

11   Indeed after I had made this suggestion, I found two references to the witch step-mother in Stith Thompson's *Motif-Index of Folk-Literature*, Copenhagen, 1956.

12   A later study, *The Cinderella Cycle* by Anna Birgitta Rooth (1951), gives more Asian versions as well as including some tales from Madagascar. While the author contests the idea of a purely Indo-European origin, she sees the four main types as products of Europe and Asia.

13   From J. B. Andrews, *Contes Ligures*, Paris, 1892, 3–7.

14   The distinction between partible and impartible inheritance is of a different kind, for even where one son inherits the 'real' property, the younger siblings usually have to be paid off, the women in dowry (see Habbakuk, 1955a, 4).

15   See Goody 1966a, 45.

16   The theme is repeated fictionally, and farcically, in Michael Arlen's *Crooked Coronet and other misrepresentations of the real facts of life*, London, 1937, which was filmed with the title 'Kind Hearts and Coronets'.

17   Joseph Jacobs, *More English Fairy Tales*, London, Nutt, 1894, from Percy, *Reliques of Ancient English Poetry*, London, 1765. (Paralleled in R. Yarington, *Two Lamentable Tragedies*, 1601; see also Halliwell's *Popular Histories*, Percy Soc., No. 18)

18   For the demographic facts see van de Walle, 1968. In India marriage also appears to be virtually universal, except in upper status groups. However, in neighbouring Tibet the role of the spinster and bachelor are well established.

19   For figures, see Mitchell, 1961, 4.

20   On women's labour see Murdock (1937b), Heath (1958), Marsh (1967) and Boserup (1970).

21   Homans 1941, 158; see the West Room of County Clare, Arensberg and Kimball, 1940, 135.

22   In Czechoslovakia, the details of the hand-over were stated with great precision. Similar detailed arrangements were made in other parts of Europe.

23   The originals of these documents are stored in the Shrine of the Book, Jerusalem, see *Inscriptions Reveal*, Israel Museum, Jerusalem, 1973, and P. Benoit, J. T. Milik and R. de Vaux, *Discoveries in the Judaean Desert*, II, Oxford, 1961.

6. Adoption in cross-cultural perspective

1   There were two lines of development here. First, Maine influenced a whole school of English law, and Vinogradoff described the kind of jurisprudence in which they were engaged as 'comparative sociology'. Second, Fustel de Coulanges was in charge of the *Ecole normale* when Durkheim was a student. Radcliffe-Brown was influenced by both these streams and in turn influenced the students who carried out the major studies of these segmentary systems; the concept of a segmentary system came straight from Durkheim's *Division of Labour* (1893).

2   Except for the tacit 'adoption' of a sister's son by a mother's brother when the latter contributes the bridewealth for his nephew's wife (Fortes, 1949, 315).

3   See also E. N. Goody, 1961, 1966, 1969.

4   Caldwell's interesting study of the support that big families in Ghana give to the aged seems based upon a certain antipathy not only to big families (as becomes a demographer) but to familial support in general. In the summary of his conclusions, he begins, 'In a society where *as yet* there is necessarily little government support for the sick and aged, old people during retirement are *forced* to rely largely on the assistance which can be provided by relatives' (1966, 22; my italics). Not only the general antifamilial sentiment but also the concept of retirement seems somewhat inappropriate for an analysis of the non-salaried sector in a society of this kind.

5   See Gaius, *Institutes*, I, 158; *Digest*, 1.7.23, *adoptio non jus sanguinis sed ius agnationis adfert*; Buckland, 1932, 122 (J. A. Crook, personal communication).

6   See for example, Ilg and Ames 1955, 342; Kornitzer 1952, 173ff.

7   This distinction is not the same as that between the adoption of minors and of adults, unless the latter is interpreted in a jural sense. Infants could easily be *sui iuris*, and adults were quite often still *alieni iuris*. The only criterion was whether you were *in potestate* still or *sui iuris* and hence an (actual or potential) head of the family yourself (J. A. Crook, personal communication).

8   Fustel de Coulanges, 1955, 55; Cicero, *Pro Domo*, 13, 14 (translated by N. H. Watts, 1923, 175); Clodius, a patrician, got himself 'adopted' by a plebeian of Rome in order to become tribune; the adoptor was already married and about 20 years of age. See also Aulus Gellius, V. 19 (transl. J. C. Rolfe, London, 1927), where the question is raised of 'whether the one who wishes to adopt is not suited to begetting children'. Crook however, suggests that 'Cicero's furious fuss about the illegality of the adoption of his enemy Clodius must not be taken too seriously, and the rules about the effect on a will of the arrival of a new son in the family by adoption imply that it was perfectly possible' (1967, 112).

9   According to Schulz (1951, 147), a man could adrogate even when he had other children, but the question would certainly be raised when considered by the *comitia curiata*. Buckland (1932, 127) states that no one who already had a child could adrogate.

10 Cicero, *De Legibus*, II, XX; for a general discussion, see J. Goody, 1962, Chapter 18. Simon Pembroke calls my attention to the fact that in the 'Lawcode' of Gortyn in Crete a man was apparently allowed to adopt even when he already had legitimate sons (Col. X, 32–XI, 23, Willetts, 1967).

11 As in Rome. Julius Caesar and Augustus were linked in this way but Crook notes that technically this procedure may not have been adoption but rather 'inheritance on condition of taking a testator's name' (1967, 112).

12 See for example, Demosthenes, 'Against Spudias'. Polyeuctus, an Athenian, had given his two daughters in marriage, one to the plaintiff and the other to a certain Leocrates, his own wife's brother. Since he had no issue, he adopted the latter as a son. But as a result of a quarrel, Leocrates severed his connection with the family, 'relinquishing his wife and with her the marriage portion' (Murray, 1936, 2).

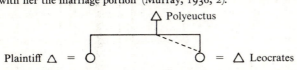

13 Fustel de Coulanges 1955, 56; see Isaeus, VI, 44 ('On the Estate of Philoctemon'); X, 11 ('Against Xenaenetus on the Estate of Aristarchus'); transl. E. S. Forster, London, 1927.

14 Demosthenes, *Private Orations*, II (transl. A. T. Murray), London, 1939.

15 Under Mitakshara law, a man may adopt a son to prevent his widow being dependent on more distant collaterals.

16 In certain parts there is also a form of adoption that applies to jural adults (*kritrima*), and another type (*dvyamushyayana*) whereby a child becomes the son of two fathers, which is used in exceptional cases as when a man intends to adopt his brother's only son.

17 Quoted by Mayne, 1892, 108–9; see also 146.

18 A widow normally adopts only on her husband's behalf, but in western India dancers can adopt a girl to follow in their profession and inherit their property (Mayne, 1892, 214). In Mithila a woman cannot adopt to her husband, but she can adopt a son as heir to herself.

19 According to Mayne, only the lower castes could adopt a son or a daughter or a sister (1892, 144); but see Madan's account of Kashmiri Brahmans for cases of such a relationship (1965).

20 Of Ramkheri in central India, Mayer writes: 'adoption tends to be within the agnatic group, especially when property is involved' (1960, 243); of the 146 land registrations, 121 were inherited from the father, 8 acquired by adoption and 17 were registered in the names of women.

21 In the Yangtze village in which Fei worked during the 1930s, 39 per cent of the unmarried girls were in this status. The author relates this high figure to the prevailing economic depression (1939, 34).

22 Rattray, 1923, 43–4; a graduated series of slave statuses is a feature of some early European codes.

23 See I. Schapera, 1956, 5.

24 In Rome and in Athens, daughters inherited as well as receiving a dowry; elsewhere it was only an heiress, i.e. a daughter without brothers, who inherited.

25 For a comment on the many (and somewhat confusing) uses of the term 'corporate group' and an attempted clarification, see J. Goody, 1961, 5.

26 In Rome and Greece citizens had to adopt citizens, so the possible mobility was only within social strata.

27 See Mayne, 1892, 77. This marriage is sometimes known by the Singhalese term, *binna*.

28 I include China among the monogamous societies because the additional women a man took were markedly inferior in status (especially ritual status, see Ch'ü, 1961, 125) and, outside rich families, concubinage was largely an alternative to adoption, a mode of begetting an heir, and as such was surrounded with restrictions. 'Concubinage was justified for the purpose of begetting an heir', writes Mrs Liu. 'One clan rule permits an heirless person over thirty years old to take a concubine, but many other clan rules give such permission only to an heirless person over forty' (1959, 70–1). In some parts of China the children of concubines had full rights of inheritance; elsewhere they were entitled to half the share of the legitimate children. But everywhere it was only the name of the senior wife that appeared on the ancestral tablets; she was the only one who was required to bring property (dowry) and the only one whose marriage was a matter of 'politics' and 'alliance'.

29 In Greece temporary expediencies were used to augment the supply of citizens after heavy military losses had been incurred (Lacey, 1968, Ch. 5).

30 A relationship between adoption and infanticide is hinted at in *Notes and Queries* (6th ed.), 1951, 73.

31 By family here I mean elementary family, since in systems where women inherit or are endowed, the conjugal unit is the critical property-holding group.

32 See the case of Aemilius Paulus (see above, 70).

33 For a similar conclusion, see Crook, 1967, 132.

34 My presentation of the African situation is necessarily schematic; there are many internal differences.

35 In non-literate societies, inheritance has to be relatively automatic; and the factor of literacy is clearly important in the African–Eurasian contrast.

36 Is the Yakö a case? Forde speaks of 'tacit adoption', but it does not appear as if the *owonen* (also called foster-child or ward) really changes his filiation in a permanent sense (Forde, 1963). In Radcliffe-Brown's introduction to *African Systems of Kinship and Marriage* (1950) there is a reference to the fact that 'in some tribes there is custom of adoption' (into the clan), but the only other mention in the index is in relation to the Swazi, where the author merely denies its existence (89).

37 Except theoretically under Islam, when the allowance of four wives has been filled. And except in special cases such as that designated 'widow concubinage' by Evans-Pritchard (1951, 92).

38 This is very clear in the Nuer case where the bridewealth for a wife who has died before producing children has to be returned to her husband's lineage (1951, 91).

39 I am referring to Evans-Pritchard's distinction between widow inheritance, where the subsequent children are affiliated to the new husband, and the levirate, where they are affiliated to the dead man (1951, 112).

40 For a discussion of 'crisis fostering', see E. N. Goody, 1966, 1969.

41 See for example Matson, 1953, 224. Ollenu writes that 'upon the death of a person control and authority over his person and property vest absolutely in his family' (1966, 68).

42 Matson points out that the Akan form of oral will (*saman-nse*) makes it possible to transmit a portion of property to a man's children, provided he has the approval of his matrilineage; such formal declarations made to the ancestors (sing. *saman*) are irrevocable. Wills, under the English Wills Act of 1837, can also be made and have some advantages, being in writing; but the law 'recognizes no restrictions on the right to dispose of self-acquired property, and by fostering secrecy allows the claims of the lineage to be defeated' (1953, 227). Commenting upon Burmese Buddhist law, Lahiri declares that 'no will could cause the devolution of property contrary to the law of inheritance' (1951, 176).

43 I would have found great difficulty in making even such a limited comparison without the help of colleagues from other fields. In particular I must thank J. A. Crook, W. K. Lacey, Maurice Freedman, Mark Elvin, Simon Pembroke, and S. J. Tambiah for helping to clarify and correct an earlier draft. I would add here that a similar picture of adoption emerges from Japan and from Burma (anyhow where Buddhist law applies).

7. *Strategies of heirship*

1 I give the figure for contemporary Germany, though even this 10 per cent is thought to be too high to be economic. Compare 80 per cent in some African countries and between 75 per cent and 80 per cent in China in 1926 (Tawney, 1932).

2 For the terminology, see M. Fortes, 1945.

3 Andrew Collver, 1963. The mean completed family size was 6.1.

4 S. Peller, 1947.

5 See J. Goody, 1972.

6 See J. Goody, 1969c, 1970a and 1971b.

7 In Europe, the term partible usually refers to the land alone, since siblings normally divide the movables of their parents and often receive compensation for not taking over

the farm. See H. J. Habbakuk, 'Family structure and economic change in nineteenth-century Europe' (1955a). For the possible influence of partible inheritance on family size, see Joan Thirsk, 'Industries in the countryside' (1961, 77), and H. E. Hallam, 'Some thirteenth century censuses' (1958).

8 See Chapter 2; the original argument appeared in J. Goody, 1969b.

9 See also Flandrin, 1975.

10 It is of course also important when a woman is inheriting property in her own right.

11 The divorce rate is calculated from the number of final divorce decrees granted under civil law, per 1,000 population. The U.A.R. figure should be compared with 2.73 for the U.S.S.R. and 2.91 for U.S.A. for the same year; it is only outdone in Puerto Rico and the Virgin Islands.

12 On the relationship between childlessness and divorce in a polygynous society, see E. Ardener (1962, 47). The initiative in divorce rests with the wife; 'the frequency of divorce among the Bakweri is determined by the readiness of the women to abscond' (79).

13 See for example, E. E. Evans-Pritchard, 1951. A man may also be required to produce an heir to his brother while the latter is still alive, if it is suspected that he cannot do this himself.

14 The turnover of marriages is socially a more important index than the divorce rate (which contributes to it), for it is more closely linked to the percentage of parentally-deficient children in the population.

15 It would be interesting to see whether this factor accounted for any aspect of the different proportions of land under the control of women in Macedonia as compared to Athens, as well as in different parts of Italy and of medieval Europe.

16 It is possible that these factors are related to the differential rates of accumulation of property by the church in various parts of Europe.

17 There were also great variations before this, anyhow in particular areas. In his study of the village of Colyton, Wrigley (1969, 87), shows that for women marrying under 30 the completed family size varied as follows:

| | | Age in years at 1st marriage: | |
		Males	Females
1560–1646	6.4	27	27
1647–1719	4.2	28	30
1720–69	4.4	26	27
1770–1837	5.9	27	25

18 This is the *cliamhan isteah* (son-in-law going in) marriage of Ireland, see C. M. Arensberg and S. T. Kimball (1940, 114). In Greece, such a marriage is known as *soghambros* (E. Friedl, 1962, 65).

19 In only one-third of these cases was the head a member of the the senior generation, which might indicate that two-thirds of farms had been the subject of pre-mortem transfer (as in Czech institution of *výměnek*) or that in those instances the parents had joined their offspring after an earlier separation on a different farm. The second alternative would be more likely to happen in the case of the wife's parents because of the age difference between husband and wife. However, pre-mortem transmission does not appear to have affected the results. Data on the actual inheritance of farms 'larger than two hectares on which married couples and older parents were living together and which had been sold to the child for a price which included a pension to the parents', showed that 81 per cent had been sold to a son (and presumably 19 per cent to a son-in-law) (Sweetser, 1964, 224). For list of references, see Sweetser, 1964.

20 I have slightly adapted these particular terms in order to point to generalised situations.

21 E. A. Weinstein, 1968.
22 See E. N. Goody, 'Kinship fostering in Gonja: deprivation or advantage?', 1969. Adoption was also absent from English law until very recently. Indeed there was no adoption even of natural offspring from the time that the claims of 'mantle-children' were rejected in the reign of Henry II (Pollock and Maitland, 1898 [1952], ii, 399).
23 On the viability of a domestic unit in relation to a particular size of herd, see Stenning, 1958.
24 For Japan, see T. C. Smith (1959, 7).
25 On this subject see also abean (1972). We find systems of temporary service, either in the house or on the land, in Albania (Hasluck, 1954) and China (Tawney, 1932).
26 For recent developments, see C. F. Westoff, R. G. Potter and P. G. Sagi (1963).
27 A. W. F. Edwards (1966, 342).
28 This is certainly true for the expressed preferences for sons against daughters, see Nancy E. Williamson, 1968.

8. Class and marriage

1 Other writers have stressed the cultural factors which they suggest make caste specific to Hindu India (e.g. Leach, 1960).
2 See, e.g. Folson's comment on the statement Bing made on p. 62 of his autobiographical account of the Nkrumah regime: 'It is equally nonsensical to include members of the National Liberation Council among the aristocratic class, whatever that means in the Ghanaian context' (Folson, 1969, 37).
3 For a discussion, see J. Goody (1963, 1969a).
4 See the discussion by Pauvert (1955).
5 On homogamy in contemporary France, see Girard (1964) who writes, 'L'homogamie apparaitrait en quelque sorte comme une corollaire de la conscience de groupe' (31). This monograph also includes a useful bibliography on the subject.
6 For further information on this kingdom, see E. N. Goody (1962, 1969, 1974) and J. Goody (1966b, 1967, 1969c).
7 A study of these marriages is being prepared by Dr Esther Goody.
8 According to Lombard (see Cornevin, 1962, 163–4).
9 Though as Merton has pointed out, in black–white marriages in the United States caste hypogamy may be crosscut by class hypergamy, as when upper black male marries lower white female.
10 Hiller (1933, 24) uses isolation device to denote arrangements and symbols which mark off in-groups from out-groups. Merton distinguishes between the isolation devices employed by subordinate groups and the exclusion devices employed by dominant groups.
11 These observations were made by Dr Enid Schildkrout in the course of her intensive investigation of urban processes in Kumasi.
12 For a recent historical review, see Mousnier (1969).
13 I.e. development rather than current distribution. Monogamy may have arisen under specific socio-economic conditions but an explanation of its present distribution cannot disregard the proselytising activities of Christian missionaries. Such considerations mean that our correlations are bound to be less than perfect.
14 The situation is somewhat different with forest crops such as bananas and taro, and with intermediary crops such as yams.
15 Other mechanical devices used in Europe were not encouraged. Indeed they were often actively discouraged. In 1844 Harris recorded the fact that two Greeks had built a water mill for the king, but it was not used because of opposition from the priests. A

generation later, a French traveler reported that the king's confessor called the mill the work of the demon and ordered it to be burned in order to destroy the spirit responsible. He excommunicated not only the builders but also anyone who had brought grain to it for milling or had eaten bread produced from its flour (Pankhurst 1961, 31).

Appendix 2

1   This correction is calculated as follows: 12.2 × 0.95 + 5.0, 22.7 × 0.95, 65.1 × 0.95.
2   These differences are reported as relating to the household, not the number of offspring. The distinction is important. For the larger size families among a higher status group in India, see M. Nag (1962, 48ff.).

References

Abraham, W. E. 1962 *The Mind of Africa*. London.

Adam, A. 1968 *Casablanca: Essai sur la transformation de la société marocaine au contact de l'Occident*. Editions du C.N.R.S., Paris.

Adams, R. McC. 1966 *The Evolution of Urban Society*. London.

Allan, W. 1965 *The African Husbandman*. Edinburgh.

Allott, A. N. 1966 The Ashanti law of property. *Zeitschrift für vergleichende Rechtwissenschaft* 68, 129–215.

Alvarez, F. 1881 *Narrative of the Portugese Embassy to Abyssinia during the Years 1520–1528* (Lord Stanley ed.). London.

Andrews, J. B. 1892 *Contes Ligures*. Paris.

Anthony, K. R. M. and Johnston, B. F. 1968 Field Study of Agricultural Change: Katsina Province. Preliminary Report no. 6, Food Research Institute, Stanford University, Stanford, Calif.

Appadorai, A. 1954 *The Status of Women in South Asia*. Bombay.

Ardener, E. 1962 *Divorce and Fertility: An African Study*. London.

Arensberg, C. M. and Kimball, S. T. 1940 *Family and Community in Ireland*. Cambridge, Mass.

Balsdon, J. P. V. D. 1962 *Roman Women: Their History and Habits*. London.

Barber, B. 1957 *Social Stratification*. New York.

Barclay, G. W. 1954 *Colonial Development and Population in Taiwan*. Princeton, N.J.

Barnes, J. A. 1954 *Politics in a Changing Society*. London.

Barton, R. F. 1949 *The Kalingas: Their Institutions and Custom Law*. Chicago.

Baumann, H. 1928 The division of work according to sex in African hoe culture. *Africa* I, 289–319.

Black, J. S. and Chrystal, G. W. 1912 *William Robertson Smith*. London.

Blalock, H. M. 1964 *Causal Inferences in Non-experimental Research*. Chapel Hill, N.C.

Bloch, M. 1966 *French Rural History*. London.

Boserup, E. 1970 *Women's Role in Economic Development*. London.

Bosman, W. 1967 *A New and Accurate Description of the Coast of Guinea, divided into the Gold, the Slave, and the Ivory Coasts* [first published 1705]. London.

Bourdieu, P. 1962 Célibat et condition paysanne. *Etudes rurales*, 5–6, 32–135.

Bracton, H. de 1569 *De Legibus* [13th century]. London.

Buckland, W. W. 1932 *A Text-Book of Roman Law* (2nd ed.). Cambridge.

Buckley, J. and Goody, J. R. 1974 Problems involved in sample selection. In *Studies in Cultural Diffusion: Galton's Problem* (J. M. Schaefer ed.). New Haven, Conn.

Burton, R. 1864 *A Mission to Gelele*. London.

Busia, K. A. 1962 *The Challenge of Africa*. New York.

Caldwell, J. C. 1966 The erosion of the family: a study of the fate of the family in Ghana. *Population Studies* 20, 5–26.

Carrasco, P. 1959 *Land and Policy in Tibet*. Seattle, Wash.

Childe, V. G. 1954a *What Happened in History* (revised edition). London.

1954b Early forms of society. In C. Singer *et al.*, (ed.), *A History of Technology*. Oxford.

Ch'ü, T.-T. 1961 *Law and Society in Traditional China* (Le Monde d'outre-mer passé et présent, Ser. 1, No. 4). Paris.

Clignet, R. 1970 *Many Wives, Many Powers*. Evanston, Ill.

Collver, A. 1963 The family cycle in India and the United States. *American Sociological Review* 28, 86–96.

Coquéry-Vidrovich, C. 1969 Recherches sur un mode de production africain. *La Pensée* 144, 61–78.

Cornevin, R. 1962 *Histoire du Dahomey*. Paris.

Coulborn, R. (ed.) 1956 *Feudalism in History*. Princeton, N.J.

Cox, M. R. 1893 *Cinderella, 345 Variants* (Folk Lore Society Monograph Series No. 31). London.

Crook, J. A. 1967 *Law and Life of Rome*. London.

Davis, K. 1941 Intermarriage in caste societies. *American Anthropoligist* 43, 376–95.

Derrett, J. P. M. 1963 *Introduction to Modern Hindu Law*. Bombay.

Dole, G. E. 1965 The lineage pattern of kinship nomenclature: its significance and development. *Southwestern Journal of Anthropology* 21, 36–62.

Dorjahn, V. 1959 The factor of polygamy in African demography. In M. Herskovits and W. Bascom (eds.) *Continuity and Change in African Cultures*. Chicago.

Driver, A. R. and Miles, J. C. 1952 *The Babylonian Laws* (2 vols.). Oxford.

Duby, G. 1962 *L'Economie rurale et la vie des campagnes dans l'occident médiéval–France, Angleterre, Empire IXe–XVe siècles: essai de synthèse et perspectives de recherches*. 2 vols. Paris.

Dumont, L. 1957 *Une Sous-Caste de l'Inde du Sud: Organisation sociale et religion des Pramalai Kallar*. Paris and The Hague.

1966 *Homo Hierarchicus*. Paris.

Durkheim, E. 1947 *The Division of Labor in Society* [1st French edition 1893]. New York.

Dyen, I. and Aberle, D. F. 1974 *Lexical Reconstruction*. Cambridge.

Edwards, A. W. F. 1966 Sex-ratio data analysed independently of family limitation. *Annals of Human Genetics*. 29, 86–96.

Eisenstadt, S. N. 1963 *The Political Systems of Empires*. New York.

Evans-Pritchard, E. E. 1940 *The Nuer*. Oxford.

1951 *Kinship and Marriage among the Nuer*. Oxford.

Fancher, H. L. 1956 The relationship between the occupational status of individuals and the sex ratio of their offspring. *Human Biology* 28, 316–22.

Fei, H. T. 1939 *Peasant Life in China*. London.

Fei, H. T. and Chang, C.-I. 1948 *Earthbound China*. London.

Flandrin, J.-L. 1969 Contraception, mariage, et relations amoureuses. *Annales E.S.C.* 24, 374–7.

1972 Mariage tardif et vie sexuelle. *Annales E.S.C.* 27, 351–78.

1975 *Les Amours paysannes (XVIe-XIXe siècle)*. Paris.

Folson, K. 1969 An African tragedy. *Encounter* 33, 35–43.

Forde, D. 1963 Unilineal fact or fiction: an analysis of the composition of kin-groups among the Yakö. In I. Shapera (ed.), *Studies in Kinship and Marriage*. London.

Fortes, M. 1945 *The Dynamics of Clanship among the Tallensi*. London.

1949a Time and social structure. In M. Fortes (ed.), *Social Structure: Studies Presented to A. R. Radcliffe-Brown*. Oxford.

1949b *The Web of Kinship among the Tallensi*. London.

1953 The structure of unilineal descent groups. *American Anthropologist* 55, 17–41.

1959 Descent, filiation and affinity. *Man* 59, 309 and 331. Reprinted in M. Fortes, *Time and Social Structure and other essays*. London, 1970.

1961 Pietas in ancestor worship: the Henry Myers lecture 1960. *Journal of the Royal Anthropological Institute* 91, 166–91.

Fustel de Coulanges, N. D. 1864 *La Cité antique* (transl. as *The ancient city*. 1874) republished as *Ancient city: a study of the religion, laws, and institutions of Greece and Rome*. New York, 1955.

Freedman, M. 1966 *Chinese Lineage and Society: Fukien and Kwangtung*. London.

(ed.) 1970 *Family and Kinship in Chinese Society*. Stanford, Calif.

Friedl, E. 1962 *Vasilika: A Village in Modern Greece*. New York.

Girard, A. 1964 *Le choix du conjoint*. Institut national d'études demographiques, Travaux et documents no. 44. Paris.

Gittelsohn, A. M. 1960 Family limitation based on family composition. *American Journal of Human Genetics* 12, 425–33.

Gluckman, M. 1950 Kinship and marriage among the Lozi of Northern Rhodesia and the Zulu of Natal. In A. R. Radcliffe-Brown and D. Forde (eds.), *African Systems of Kinship and Marriage*. London.

Goode, W. J. 1963 *World Revolution and Family Patterns*. New York.

Goody, E. N. 1961 Kinship, marriage and the developmental cycle among the Gonja of Northern Ghana. Ph.D. thesis, University of Cambridge.

1962 Conjugal separation and divorce among the Gonja of Northern Ghana. In M. Fortes (ed.) *Marriage in Tribal Societies*. Cambridge.

1966 Fostering in Ghana: a preliminary survey. *Ghana Journal of Sociology* 2, 26–33.

1969 Kinship fostering in Gonja: deprivation or advantage? In P. Mayer (ed.), *Socialization: The Approach from Social Anthropology*. London.

1971 Forms of pro-parenthood: The sharing and substitution of parental roles. In J. Goody (ed.), *Kinship*. London.

1974 *Contexts of Kinship*. Cambridge.

Goody, J. R. 1956 *The Social Organisation of the LoWiili*. London.

1958 The fission of domestic groups among the LoDagaba. In J. R. Goody (ed.), *The Developmental Cycle in Domestic Groups*. Cambridge.

1959 The mother's brother and the sister's son in West Africa. *Journal of the Royal Anthropological Institute* 89, 61–88.

1961 The classification of double descent systems. *Current Anthropology* 2, 3–25. Reprinted in *Comparative Studies in Kinship*. London and Stanford, 1969.

1962 *Death, Property and the Ancestors*. London and Stanford.

1963 Feudalism in Africa? *Journal of African History* 4, 1–18.

1966a Introduction to J. R. Goody (ed.), *Succession to High Office*. Cambridge.

1966b Rotational succession among the Gonja. In J. R. Goody (ed.), *Succession to High Office*. Cambridge.

1967 The over-kingdom of Gonja. In D. Forde and P. Kaberry (eds.), *West African Kingdoms*. London.

1969a Economy and feudalism in Africa. *Economic History Review* 22, 393–405.

1969b Inheritance, property and marriage in Africa and Eurasia. *Sociology* 3, 55–76.

1969c Succession in contemporary Africa. *Archives Européennes de Sociologie* 10, 27–40.

1969d Marriage policy and incorporation in Northern Ghana. In *Comparative Studies in Kinship*. London.

1970a Sideways or downwards? *Man* 5, 627–38.

1970b Cousin terms. *Southwestern Journal of Anthropology* 26, 125–42.

1971a Class and marriage in Africa and Eurasia. *American Journal of Sociology* 76, 585–603.

1971b *Technology, Tradition and the State in Africa.* London.

1972 The evolution of the family. In P. Laslett and R. Wall (eds.), *Household and Family in Past Time.* Cambridge.

1973 Bridewealth and dowry in Africa and Eurasia. In J. R. Goody and S. J. Tambiah, *Bridewealth and Dowry.* Cambridge.

1976 Aging in non-industrial societies. In J. R. Birren, E. Shanes and R. Binstock (eds.), *Handbook of Aging and the Social Sciences.* New York.

Goody, J. R. *et al.* 1971 Causal inferences concerning inheritance and property. *Human Relations* 4, 295–314.

Goody, J. R. and Buckley, J. Inheritance and Woman's Labour in Africa. *Africa* 43, 108–21.

Goody, J. R. and Tambiah, S. J. 1973 *Bridewealth and Dowry.* Cambridge.

Graham, H. G. 1937 *The Social Life of Scotland in the Eighteenth Century* [first published 1899]. London.

Graves, T. D., Graves, N. B. and Kobrin, M. J. 1969 Historical inferences from Guttman Scales: the return of age-area magic. *Current Anthropology* 10, 317–38.

Gray, J. 1965 *The Legacy of Canaan* (2nd ed.). London.

Grove, A. T. 1957 *Land and Population in Katsina Province.* Kaduna.

1961 Population densities and agriculture in Northern Nigeria. In K. M. Barbour and R. M. Prothero (eds.), *Essays on African Population.* London.

Grundy, K. W. 1964 The class struggle in Africa: an examination of conflicting theories. *Journal of Modern African Studies* 2, 379–93.

Habbakuk, H. J. 1950 Marriage settlement in the eighteenth century. *Transactions of the Royal Historical Society* 32, 15–30.

1955a Family structure and economic change in nineteenth-century Europe. *Journal of Ecclesiastical History* 15, 1–12.

1955b Daniel Finch, second earl of Nottingham: his house and estate. In J. H. Plumb (ed.), *Studies in Social History.* London.

Hadden, K. and DeWalt, B. 1974 Path analysis: some anthropological examples. *Ethnology* 13, 105–28.

Hahn, E. 1896 *Die Haustiere und ihre Beziehungen zur Wirtschaft des Menschen.* Leipzig.

Hair, P. E. H. 1966 Bridal pregnancy in rural England in earlier centuries. *Population Studies* 20, 233–43.

Hajnal, J. 1965 European marriage patterns in perspective. In D. V. Glass and D. E. C. Eversley (eds.), *Population in History.* London.

Hallam, H. E. 1958 Some thirteenth century censuses. *Economic History Review* 10, 340–61.

Hasluck, M. 1954 *The Unwritten Law in Albania.* Cambridge.

Heath, D. B. 1958 Sexual division of labor and cross-cultural research. *Social Forces* 37, 77–9.

Hiller, E. T. 1933 *Principles of Sociology.* New York.

Hole, F. and Flannery, K. V. 1967 The prehistory of south-western Iran: a preliminary report. *Proceedings of the Prehistoric Society* 33, 147–206.

Hollingshead, A. B. 1950 Cultural factors in the selection of marriage mates. *American Sociological Review* 15, 619–27.

Hollingsworth, T. H. 1964–5 Demography of the British peerage. *Population Studies,* 18, Supplement, November.

Holmes, G. A. 1957 *The Estates of the Higher Nobility in Fourteenth Century England.* Cambridge.

Homans, G. C. 1941 *English Villagers of the Thirteenth Century*. Cambridge, Mass. 1951 *The Human Group*. London.

Hsu, F. L. K. 1949 *Under the Ancestor's Shadow*. London.

Ilg, F. E. and Ames, L. B. 1955 *Child Behavior*. New York.

Jacobs, J. 1894 *More English Fairy Tales*. London.

James, T. E. 1957 The illegitimate and deprived child: legitimation and adoption. In *A Century of Family Law, 1857–1957* (R. H. Graveson and F. R. Crane, eds.), London.

Johnson, E. L. 1965 *Family Law* (2nd ed.). London.

Juvenal. 1967 *The Sixteen Satires*. Transl. by P. Green. London.

Kaberry, P. 1957 Primitive states. *British Journal of Sociology* 8, 224–34.

Kapadia, K. M. 1966 *Marriage and the Family in India* (3rd ed.). Bombay.

Köbben, A. J. F. 1967 Why exceptions? The logic of cross-cultural analysis. *Current Anthropology* 8, 3–34.

Kornitzer, M. 1952 *Child Adoption in the Modern World*. London.

Lacey, W. K. 1968 *The Family in Classical Greece*. London.

Lahiri, S. C. 1951 *Principles of Modern Buddhist Law* (5th ed.). Calcutta.

Land, A. 1893 Introduction. In M. Cox, *Cinderella, 345 Variants*. London.

Laslett, P. 1969 Size and structure of the household in England over three centuries. *Population Studies* 23, 199–233.

Leach, E. R. 1947 Cultural change with special reference to the hill tribes of Burma and Assam. Ph.D. Thesis, University of London.

1954 *Political Systems of Highland Burma*. London.

1960 *Aspects of Caste in South India, Ceylon, and Northwest Pakistan*. Cambridge.

Levine, D. N. 1965 *Wax and Gold*. Chicago.

Lévi-Strauss, C. 1949 *Les Structures élémentaires de la parenté*. Paris and The Hague.

Lewis, O. 1958 *Village Life in Northern India*. New York.

Liu, H.-C. W. 1959 *The Traditional Chinese Clan Rules* (Monographs of the Association for Asian Studies, No. 7). New York.

Llyn, C. W. 1942 Agriculture in North Mamprussi: a review of a decade's progress. *Farm and Forest* 3, 78–83.

Lowie, R. H. 1937 *The History of Ethnological Theory*. London.

McLennan, J. F. 1857 Law. *Encyclopaedia Britannica* vol. 13, 253–79. 1970 *Primitive Marriage* (ed. P. Rivière). Chicago [1st ed. 1865].

McNeill, W. H. 1963 *The Rise of the West*. Chicago.

McQuitty, L. L. 1960 Hierarchical linkage analysis for the isolation of types. *Educational Psychological Measurement* 20, 55–67.

Madan, T. N. 1965 *Family and Kinship: A Study of the Pandits of Rural Kashmir*. Bombay.

Maine, H. S. 1931 *Ancient Law* (1st ed., 1861). London.

Malinowski, B. 1922 *Argonauts of the Western Pacific*. London.

Mallowan, M. E. L. 1965 *Early Mesopotamia and Iran*. London.

Marsh, R. M. 1967 *Comparative Sociology*. New York.

Martinez-Alier, V. 1972 Elopement and seduction in nineteenth-century Cuba. *Past and Present* 55, 91–129.

1974 *Marriage, Class and Colour in Nineteenth Century Cuba*. Cambridge.

Matson, J. N. 1953 Testate succession in Ashanti. *Africa* 23, 224–32.

Mayer, A. 1960 *Caste and Kinship in Central India*. Berkeley and Los Angeles.

Mayne, J. D. 1892 *A Treatise on Hindu Law and Usage* (5th ed.; 1st ed. 1878). London.

Mellaart, J. 1961 Roots in the soil. In S. Piggott (ed.), *The Dawn of Civilization*. London. 1967 *Çatal Hüyük: a Neolithic Town in Anatolia*. London.

Merton, R. 1941 Intermarriage and the social structure: fact and theory. *Psychiatry* 4, 361–74.

Reprinted in R. L. Coser (ed.), *The Family: Its Structure and Its Functions*. New York, 1964.

Michel, A. 1972 *Sociologie de la famille et du mariage*. Paris.

Mitchell, J. C. 1961 Social change and the stability of marriage in Northern Rhodesia. In A. Southall (ed.), *Social Change in Modern Africa*. Oxford.

Morgan, L. H. 1871 *Systems of Consanguinity and Affinity of the Human Family* (Smithsonian Contributions to Knowledge, 17, Washington, D.C.)

Mousnier, R. 1969 *Les Hiérarchies sociales de 1450 à nos jours*. Paris.

Murdock, G. P. 1937a Correlations of matrilineal and patrilineal institutions. In G. P. Murdock (ed.), *Studies in the Science of Society*. New Haven, Conn.

1937b Comparative data on division of labor by sex. *Social Forces* 15, 551–3.

1949 *Social Structure*. New York.

1959 *Africa: its People and their Culture History*. New York.

(ed.) 1960 *Social Structure in Southeast Asia*. Chicago.

1967 Ethnographic atlas: a summary. *Ethnology* 6, 109–236.

Murray, A. T. (transl.) 1936 *Demosthenes: Private Orations*, vol. I. London and Cambridge, Mass.

1939 *Demosthenes–Private Orations*, vol. II. London and Cambridge, Mass.

Nadel, S. F. 1942 *A Black Byzantium*. London.

1957 *The Theory of Social Structure*. London.

Nag, M. 1952 *Factors Affecting Human Fertility in Nonindustrial Societies*. New Haven, Conn.

Nimkoff, M. F. and Middleton, R. 1960 Types of family and types of economy. *American Journal of Sociology* 46, 215–25.

Notes and Queries on Anthropology (6th ed.) 1951 Royal Anthropological Institute, London.

Nyerere, J. 1962 'Ujamaa': The Basis of African Socialism. Reprinted in 'Ujamaa'. *Essays on Socialism* (1968). Dar es Salaam.

Ollenu, N. A. 1966 *The Law of Testate and Intestate Succession in Ghana*. London.

Pankhurst, R. 1961a Status, division of labour and employment in nineteenth-century and early twentieth-century Ethiopia. *Ethnological Society Bulletin* (University College of Addis Ababa) 2, 6–58.

1961b *An Introduction to the Economic History of Ethiopia*. London.

Parsons, T. 1954 The incest taboo in relation to social structure and the socialization of the child. *British Journal of Sociology* 5, 101–17.

1964 The place of force in social process. In H. Eckstein (ed.), *Internal War*. New York.

1966 *Societies in Evolutionary and Comparative Perspectives*. Englewood Cliffs, N.J.

Patai, R. 1959 *Sex and Family in the Bible and the Middle East*. Garden City, N.Y.

Pauvert, J.-C. 1955 Le problème des classes sociales en Afrique équatoriale. *Cahiers internationaux de sociologie* 19, 76–91.

Peller, S. 1947 Man's reproductive activity. *Bulletin of the History of Medicine* 21, 51–65.

Peristiany, J. G. (ed.) 1965 *Honour and Shame: the Values of Mediterranean Society*. London.

Pollock, Sir F. and Maitland, F. W. 1898 *History of English Law*, 2nd ed. [reprinted 1952]. Cambridge.

Postan, M. 1950 Some economic evidence of declining population in the later Middle Ages. *Economic History Review* (n.s.) 2, 221–46.

Potekhin, I. I. 1963 Land relations in African countries. *Journal of Modern African Studies* 1, 39–59.

Radcliffe-Brown, A. R. 1950 Introduction to A. R. Radcliffe-Brown and D. Forde (eds.), *African Systems of Kinship and Marriage*. London.

1952 *Structure and Function in Primitive Society*. London.

1957 *A Natural Science of Society*. New York.

Rattray, R. S. 1923 *Ashanti*. London.

Redfield, R. 1934 *Chan Kom: A Maya Village*. Washington, D.C.

Redwar, H. W. H. 1909 *Comments on Some Ordinances of the Gold Coast Colony*. London.

Rivière, P. 1970 Introduction to J. F. McLennan, *Primitive Marriage*. Chicago.

Robertson Smith, W. 1907 *Kinship and Marriage in Early Arabia*. London.

Rooth, A. B. 1951 *The Cinderella Cycle*. Lund.

Sabean, D. 1972 Famille et tenure paysanne: aux origines de la guerre des paysans en Allemagne (1525). *Annales E.S.C.* 27, 903–22.

Schapera, I. 1956 *Government and Politics in Tribal Societies*. London.

Schneider, D. M. and Gough, K. 1961 *Matrilineal Kinship*. Berkeley and Los Angeles.

Schulz, F. 1951 *Classical Roman Law*. Oxford.

Siegel, S. 1956 *Nonparametric Statistics for the Behavioral Sciences*. New York.

Smith, T. C. 1959 *The Agrarian Origins of Modern Japan*. Stanford, Calif.

Sonquist, J. A. and Morgan, J. N. 1964 *The Detection of Interaction Effects* (Survey Research Center Monograph No. 35, Institute for Social Research, University of Michigan). Ann Arbor, Mich.

Sonquist, J. A., Baker, E. L., and Morgan, J. N. 1973 *Searching for Structure* (Survey Research Center, Institute for Social Research, University of Michigan). Ann Arbor, Mich.

Southall, A. 1956 *Alur Society*. Cambridge.

Starcke, C. N. 1894 *The Primitive Family* [first German ed. 1888]. New York.

Stenning, D. J. 1958 Household viability among the pastoral Fulani. In J. R. Goody (ed.) *The Developmental Cycle in Domestic Groups*. Cambridge.

Stephens, W. N. 1962 *The Oedipus Complex*. New York.

Stone, L. 1960–1 Marriage among the English nobility in the 16th and 17th centuries. *Comparative Studies in Society and History* 3, 182–206.

    1967 *The Crisis of the Aristocracy, 1558–1641*. London.

Sweetser, D. A. 1964 Urbanization and the patrilineal transmission of farms in Finland. *Acta Sociologica* 7, 215–24.

Tawney, R. H. 1932 *Land and Labour in China*. London.

Thirsk, J. 1961 Industries in the countryside. In F. J. Fischer (ed.), *Essays in the Economic and Social History of Tudor and Stuart England*. Cambridge.

Thompson, E. P. 1972 'Rough music': le Charivari anglais. *Annales E.S.C.* 27, 285–312.

Thompson, S. 1956 *Motif-Index of Folk-Literature*. Copenhagen.

Thrupp, S. L. 1948 *The Merchant Class of Medieval London, 1300–1500*. Chicago.

Tillion, G. 1966 *Le Harem et les cousins*. Paris.

Trasler, G. B. 1960 *In Place of Parents*. London.

Ts'ao H.-C. 1958 *Dream of the Red Chamber* (transl. Chi-Chen Wang). New York.

Tylor, E. B. 1889 On a method of investigating the development of institutions: applied to laws of marriage and descent. *Journal of the Anthropological Institute* 18, 245–69. Reprinted in F. W. Moore (ed.) *Readings in Cross-Cultural Methodology*. New Haven, Conn., 1966, 1–25.

van der Sprenkel, S. 1962 *Legal Institutions in Manchu China* (L.S.E. Monographs on Social Anthropology, No. 24). London.

Van der Valk, M. H. 1956 *Conservation in modern Chinese Family law*. Studia et documenta ad iura Orientis antiqui pertinentia, Vol. 4. Leiden.

van de Walle, E. 1968 Fertility in Nigeria. In W. Brass *et al.*, *The Demography of Tropical Africa*. Princeton, N.J.

Vinogradoff, P. 1920 *Outlines of Historical Jurisprudence* vol. 1. London.

Wake, C. S. 1967 *The Development of Marriage and Kinship*. R. Needham (ed.) [first published 1889]. Chicago.

Weinstein, E. A. 1968 Adoption. *International Encyclopaedia of the Social Sciences*. New York.

Westermarck, E. 1921 *The History of Human Marriage* (5th ed.). London.

Westoff, C. F., Potter, R. G. and Sagi, P. G. 1963 *The Third Child: a Study in the Prediction of Fertility*. Princeton, N.J.

Wilks, I. 1975 *Asante in the Nineteenth Century*. Cambridge.

Willetts, R. F. 1967 The law code of Gortyn. *Kadmos*, suppl. 1. Berlin.

Williamson, N. E. 1968 Preference for sons around the world. Harvard School of Public Health (MS.)

Workneh, Y. 1961 An essay on community life. *Ethnological Society Bulletin* (University College of Addis Ababa) 2, 82–91.

Wrigley, E. A. 1969 *Population and History*. London.

Yang, M. C. 1947 *A Chinese Village: Taitou, Shantung Province*. London.

Index